CANAL WALKS

Boatman's-eye view up the staircase locks at Foxton (Walk 3)

Canal Walks
Vol 2. Midlands

by
Dennis Needham

CICERONE PRESS
MILNTHORPE, CUMBRIA

© Dennis Needham, 1997
ISBN 1 85284 225 3
A catalogue record for this book is available
from the British Library.

© All photographs by Elizabeth Fowler

Dedication
For Lel, Att and Gav, three good "kids"

Advice to Readers

Readers are advised that whilst every effort is taken by the author
to ensure the accuracy of this guidebook, changes can occur which
may affect the contents. It is advisable to check locally on transport,
accommodation, shops etc. but even rights-of-way can be altered
and, more especially overseas, paths can be eradicated by landslip,
forest fires or changes of ownership.

The publisher would welcome notes of any such changes.

Cicerone books by the same author:
　　　Canal Walks Vol 1: North
　　　Canal Walks Vol 3: South

Front cover: On the Shropshire Union Canal

CONTENTS

INTRODUCTION

Canal towpath walking. The ultimate escape into a world that has changed little in over 200 years. The routes and infrastructure are virtually as conceived. Only their users have altered.

The towpaths alongside most of England's canal system were originally built for use by horses, the initial motive power for boats. Most of our canals were constructed within thirty years either side of 1800, and provided cheap bulk transport at a time when this was unknown. Although much faster than the horse and cart, and able to carry a vastly greater tonnage, the canals themselves fell victim to the search for increased speed and efficiency. Nineteenth century railways offered a more rapid service with much greater flexibility. With the arrival waterside of steam, soon followed by diesel power, the need for horse towpaths lessened and, in common with the accompanying water, maintenance was neglected.

Gradually falling into disuse, canals started to close. Many are now gone, leaving hardly a trace of their existence. However, soon after the last war, the Inland Waterways Association was founded to fight for the retention of these lengths of history. Under the enlightened leadership of Robert Aikman, campaigns to save threatened canals were mounted with a great degree of success. At that time, officialdom regarded canals as redundant and best filled in. Attending many public enquiries concerning the fate of these abandoned waterways, Aikman was able to demonstrate that it was cheaper to restore a canal than to infill it. This was not occasioned by financial legerdemain, but by arguing hard facts.

The renaissance of canals for recreational use has seen miles of towpaths reinstated, and they now provide hundreds of miles of good walking. Indeed, British Waterways themselves are responsible for over 1,500 miles, virtually all in reasonable condition. A generation ago the phrase "down by the canal" had connotations of grimy, rat-ridden old warehouses in the seedy part of town. Now, enlightened action by local and national bodies, both statutory and voluntary, often aided by local authorities, have transformed them - and our perception - into corridors of green, passing through some of the most beautiful scenery in this green and pleasant land, whilst giving city dwellers linear parks in which to linger.

From Essex to Lancashire, Yorkshire to Somerset, this great heritage is available to anyone who is able to walk for a couple of hours. There are no steep hills, although on some walks they crowd the water, almost giving the impression of fell walking. Equipped with nothing more than a pair of stout shoes - and the inevitable waterproof - they are there and available. Their very nature as one-time transport arteries means that, although there are miles of greenery, the walks are never too far away from civilisation and its attendant public transport. This gives the walker the opportunity to head away from his/her car, confident that after a delightful and invigorating one-way walk, bus or train will return him/her to the car park.

This book follows a simple format. You are guided from a basepoint towards public transport that will convey you to the far end of the walk. From there, a walk back to the start can be undertaken at whatever pace suits. This eliminates the possibility of having to wait hours for the transport at the far end, to say nothing of the situation that once faced this writer when, after nine miles, the local bus drivers were found to be on strike. There are six circular walks, and a couple that do use transport for the return leg. There is always a good reason, and it is given in the text.

Most walks start at a point convenient to public transport and a car park. An Ordnance Survey grid reference is quoted for this location. A fact panel provides all the information needed before departure. Allow at least an hour for every two miles; there is always a view or building that simply demands a halt. Walks are grouped into chapters according to their area. The title "Midlands" is a liberal interpretation, allowing the writer vast scope to select the finest walks available. Contrast the stark industrial dereliction of central Birmingham with the delicate water meadows of the Nene at Oundle. The majesty of Royal Leamington Spa and the country homeliness of Cropredy. All are visited within these covers.

Pause and admire tunnels dug through solid rock without the aid of a single power tool, and delight at stone or brick built bridges, built for no other purpose than to allow farmers access to their fields that were severed when the canal was cut. This is even enshrined in the name of one bridge, although today Farmers Bridge is actually in the very centre of Birmingham. Natural beauty is everywhere. Although many of the walks either begin or end in a town, there are miles of the most delightful countryside between: Derbyshire's Peak District, the hunting shires of Leicester, the mighty Severn valley or charming Northamptonshire villages. On a more bucolic note, a cow leisurely chewing its cud, peering over the parapet of a bridge, seems to add another dimension to canal walking.

Cities create their own fascination from the towpath. Birmingham, England's second city, is a fine example of "The Canal Effect". In a large city, the canal makes its entry through the back door, virtually ignored by residents. How many people who live in central Birmingham know that kingfishers, cormorants and kestrels live within a mile of New Street station? They do and the walker is the most likely to see this manifestation. On the mammal side, fox and mink are city dwellers now; again, few people know.

This life is multiplied in the country. The scars of construction are now long gone, and many canals have a timeless feel to them. A full range of water fowl will be seen on canals, whilst rabbit, stoat, water vole and squirrel have taken up residence bankside. There is flora in abundance, many wild fruiting bushes and trees and enough butterflies to keep any lepidopterist in ecstasy. All canalside. Camera, binoculars and a bird identification book are all useful extras to a canal walk.

The OS Landranger series are invaluable maps for this kind of walking, but there are also canal cruising guides available. Usually at a scale of two inches to a mile, much of the information crammed between the covers is, perhaps, more relevant to boaters. But the walks will surely be augmented. Robert Nicholson Publications offer *The Ordnance Survey Guide to the Waterways* in five parts. Most of the walks in this book are to be found in the "Central" edition, with the "South" and "The Broads and Fens" covering the remainder. Waterways World *Canal Guides* also offer invaluable snippets.

Although the walks are never too remote, the basic safety items carried by most sensible walkers are never out of place: compass, first aid, warm clothing, waterproofs, drink and a little energy food all fit into the smallest backpack, allowing the walker to face any situation with quiet confidence. One delightful aspect of these walks is that they pass a range of very congenial pubs. Many are still quite basic but most offer food, and the beer always seems more palatable after a good walk.

As curiosity and interest is aroused by the waterways - as it surely will be - there are a number of books that will increase your knowledge. The most comprehensive coverage of history is recorded in a series of books by Charles Hadfield, published by David and Charles (of which Hadfield was once the "Charles"). Many are out

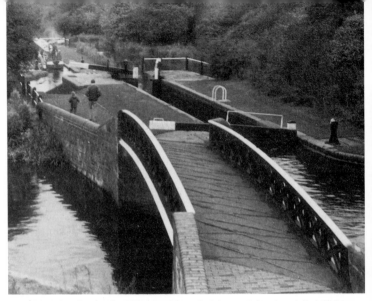

The Delph Nine Locks. Water leaving to the left once led to the original flight.
(Walk 29)

of print now, but still obtainable through libraries. Three monthly magazines currently cover the subject: *Waterways World* caters for the more serious enthusiast, but in a very readable style; *Canal and Riverboat* takes a less traditional approach to the subject and is easily read; *Canal Boat* is the most visually attractive. All these titles publish a canalside walk each month.

Finally, do not neglect the "green" aspect of canalside walking. Canals are man-made, although, 200 years along, it is difficult to believe. Towpaths were constructed to withstand the steady plod of thousands of horses, day in and day out. Accordingly, they do not show the kind of wear that is causing so much concern in many of our more popular walking areas. There is a warm satisfaction in knowing that after a good walk which has brought exercise, pleasure and fine scenery, you can retire to the fireside confident that your boots have done not the slightest damage to an otherwise frail environment. A comforting thought indeed.

So, lace up those boots, and try any of these thirty carefully selected walks. Then see how long it is before you are well and truly hooked on towpath walking.

Chapter 1:
Oxfordshire, Northamptonshire and Leicestershire

WALK 1 - BANBURY TO CROPREDY - OXFORD CANAL

Although one of our older canals, the Oxford is not an easy one to walk as it stays remote from centres of population, thus making the organisation of return transport problematical.

The Oxford Canal was opened throughout in 1790. Its prime purpose was to provide a link between the Midlands - particularly the coalfields - and London via the River Thames. James Brindley was the engineer and the canal carries his trademark: long winding loops more intent on holding a contour than with time and efficiency. The great man died in 1772, only three years after the Act was granted, and much of the actual construction was undertaken by his successor, Samuel Simcox. He completed the work from Coventry to Banbury by 1778, but the remaining 27 miles to Oxford were not finished until 1790 with Robert Whitworth as engineer.

Trade flowed immediately, and good times were enjoyed by the shareholders: but not for long. The Grand Junction Canal from London to Braunston - see Walk 2 - was completed. This shortened the journey time to the capital dramatically, and the southern Oxford lost much of its trade. Then came the Napton to Birmingham Canal which shortened the journey to the north, and the northern Oxford also lost out. Paradoxically, this falling of trade did not result in much revenue loss.

Between Napton and Braunston were $5^{1}/_{2}$ miles of Oxford water. For the privilege of saving time, boats paid a toll that was almost extortion. This kept the Oxford profitable for years. They carried out modernisation work on the northern section, reducing the journey from 36 to 22 miles, and straightened out a mass of curves near Braunston. However the southern section was relatively untouched, and remains today as the finest example of a contour canal to be found in this country.

BEFORE YOU START

WALK DISTANCE:	5½ miles
MAP:	OS Landranger Series No 151
START:	The Brasenose Arms, Cropredy, 2 miles east of the A423 Southam to Banbury road
PUBLIC TRANSPORT:	All services to Banbury - local bus from there
STARTING GRID REF:	SP 468468
CAR PARKING:	Side streets locally
TRANSPORT:	Fragmented. All services leave in the morning, more on some days than others. Stagecoach Midland Red services 509 and 510 provide the main ones - 01295 262368. Jeffs Coaches run an occasional service 510: 01295 768292. Banbury Community Transport - 01295 255863 - operate from the VG Stores in the village on Tuesdays whilst Geoff Amos Coaches - 01327 702181 - operate from the VG Stores on Thursday and Saturday
REFRESHMENT:	Pubs and shops in Cropredy, everything in Banbury, nothing between
NEAREST TIC:	8 Horsefair, Banbury, Oxfordshire OX16 0AA - 01295 259855

THE WALK

The bus picks up outside the Brasenose Arms and terminates in Banbury bus station. Across the parking area is the canal, which can be reached down the lane to the right of the station. Cross the wooden lift bridge, the only manifestation of this delightful design on this section of the walk, and turn left.

Banbury to M42 Bridge - 2½ miles

You arrive immediately at the first lock. This area was once entirely devoted to the canal. To the right was a large warehouse that burnt down in relatively recent times, whilst the bus station itself was built on what was the canal basin. It was a beautifully remote area, albeit somewhat run-down when the council decided to infill in the early 1960s. Unfortunately, subsequent development of the waterside leaves a lot to be desired in terms of incorporating the canal into an attractive environment, and much could be learnt from other towns and cities around the country.

By the first bridge is the sole remaining piece of Banbury waterway heritage: Tooley's Yard. In 1993 plans were laid by a property Trust to redevelop the whole area, despite the Ancient Monument status of the boatyard. Cherwell District Council passed plans to turn it into "a focus for eating places", although the yard has been retained for the time being. The outcry from boaters, boaters' organisations and local residents has caused a rethink.

So what is Tooley's? In hard terms it is a decrepit old boatyard and dry dock in the centre of a town. But its place in boating lore is far more significant. It was opened around 1779 and is seen as the place where the leisure boating revolution began. Operated by the Tooley family until the last descendant, Herbert, died in the early 1980s, it was the place where Tom Rolt adapted his boat *Cressy* for residential use. The publication of his book *Narrow Boat* in 1944 opened the eyes of the country to the possibilities of leisure use for the inland waterways.

Under Spiceball Bridge and a large park to the right runs towards the River Cherwell, giving open space to the town. Beyond bridge 162 the canal's course was altered late in the 1970s. The

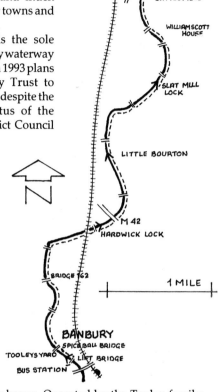

current line curves away to the right whilst a now weeded section carries straight on. The towpath passes under a concrete road lies just beyond the canal, and stays there for a few hundred yards before the canal turns right again and follows a straight line - something not usual on the Oxford - towards a railway bridge.

Behind the canal to the right was once a quite important railway junction. It arrived from Woodford Halse, a hamlet 8 miles to the north-west, which was the nearest point that the Great Central Railway got to the Great Western. The Great Central was the last main line built in this country, opening in 1900 to link London Marylebone with Rugby, Leicester, Nottingham, Sheffield and Manchester, with branches to Bradford. It provided a vital freight - and passenger - link between Yorkshire and the south coast of England via Reading and Basingstoke. Woodford Halse was a pure railway town, a much more modern manifestation of this phenomenon than say Crewe or Swindon. Now the iron horse has gone, and the acres of sidings, engine sheds and station with it.

Under the bridge is Hardwick lock, followed by the motorway crossing noisily overhead.

M42 Bridge to Cropredy - 3 miles

With the motorway behind, the walk assumes a very rural feel. The Cherwell valley continues to the right, and the railway is never too far away to the left, but, essentially, this is rolling Oxfordshire countryside at its very best.

The towpath winds along, past Little Bourton and Slat Mill locks before trees on the right, across the valley mark Williamscott House. These trees then reach to the towpath before a sharp left turn starts the canal on the last straight length to Cropredy. Leave by the bridge, turn left and walk back to the pub.

Cropredy village has become best known in recent times for the Folk Music Festival held there. Its first claim to fame was when the river bridge, a few hundred yards to the right of the canal, became the site of an important Civil War battle. In 1644 King Charles' army was travelling from Oxford when they met Cromwell's forces under General Waller at the bridge. Despite an overwhelming superiority of numbers the General failed to defeat the Royalist cavalry. Some of the soldiers who died in the battle are buried at St.

Mary the Virgin church in the village. A mark on the vestry floor there is believed to be a bloodstain from a young messenger who was killed on that spot after the battle.

A beautiful horse chestnut tree that stands on the village green was planted in 1897 to mark the silver jubilee of Queen Victoria, and a curiosity in the village is the Curfew Bell, still rung on three evenings each week.

WALK 2 - BRAUNSTON TO WEEDON - GRAND UNION CANAL

Braunston was once the hub of long distance canal carrying in England. Its junction, where the Grand Junction - later the Grand Union - joined the Oxford, was where coal carrying boats from the Warwickshire coalfield met the manufacturing cargoes travelling to and from Birmingham.

The Grand Union Canal was formed as recently as 1929, an amalgamation of all the canals between London and Birmingham with many smaller branches. But by far the major component was the Grand Junction Company. This had started life building the line between the Thames at Brentford and Braunston. A major achievement in its day, the canal was the first north/south canal that had to cross two watersheds in its 93 mile run. The long climb out of London over the Chilterns was followed by a descent into the Ouse valley. Then a climb to Buckby before plunging down again en route to the Avon valley. It was constructed as a barge canal (14ft wide locks), and built to a very high standard. As the main transport artery between England's capital and the second city, it was a very busy line, actually carrying regular freight until 1969. This was coal, travelling along the northern section of the Oxford to Braunston and then down to a factory on the outskirts of London. After the amalgamation in 1929, a major upgrading was undertaken with government money in an attempt to secure freight along the Grand Union. The northern section - from Napton to Birmingham - had been built with 7ft locks. These were rebuilt - see Walk 19 - along with major dredging and bank protection work undertaken on the Grand Junction further south.

One of several old relics outside the shop on Braunston lock flight

But to no avail. Before any real benefits could be seen, the war started and plans to replace narrowboats with barges and widen the Leicester arm were stillborn. With it went the last hope that inland waterway carrying could be sustained, and the trend from 1945 onwards was one of ever reducing trade. This was exacerbated by nationalisation in 1948. The British Transport Commission, charged with operating all surface transport, clearly saw the canals as obsolete, and an aggressive programme of transferring freight to their rail and road services started. Canals were even more neglected than they had been prior to the war and many lost their trade during this period, including some of the Grand Union branches.

With small independent carriers starting business on the Grand Union in an attempt to keep some freight, this main line was never seriously threatened with closure. Enthusiasts-cum-businessmen made valiant attempts against the odds to keep trade on the water. With coal usage, the staple cargo, dwindling, it was a vain struggle in one respect, but their actions ensured that the goods carrying and leisure ages overlapped, and the Grand Union moved seamlessly between the two. The recent carrying history is evidenced in this area by the gaggle of old working boats always to be found. Whilst some have been converted for living afloat, there are a few still left, like spectres from another age, waiting endlessly for the work that will never come.

This walk has only become possible in recent years. After the demise of horse drawn boats, the towpaths were allowed to decay, and this one, particularly along the summit level, was impassable for years. Then, conscious of the rapid increase in towpath walking, British Waterways started working with local councils to reinstate them. This section was completed as part of a high profile long distance footpath between London and Birmingham. This 145 mile walk was opened, to great acclaim, in 1993 to the benefit of everyone from the 10 minute stroller before a pub visit through to the dedicated walker, many of whom do walk the whole length.

BEFORE YOU START

WALK DISTANCE:	9 miles
MAP:	OS Landranger Series No 152
START:	High Street, Weedon. This is the A45 Northampton to Coventry road
PUBLIC TRANSPORT:	Northampton and Rugby are the nearest points
STARTING GRID REF:	SP 630590
CAR PARKING:	Roadside lay-by, or (with permission) there are a couple of pubs in the village
TRANSPORT:	Stagecoach United Counties service X64 from Corby to Birmingham calls in Weedon and at Braunston Turn
REFRESHMENT:	Pubs at each end, several between. Range of shops at Braunston, more limited in Weedon. Refreshment type shops en route at Braunston bottom lock, Braunston top lock, Buckby Wharf and Whilton bottom lock
NEAREST TIC:	Moot Hall, Market Square, Daventry, Northants NN11 4BH - 01327 300277

THE WALK

The bus stop is near the crossroads where the A45 and A5 intersect. Alight at the Boatman in Braunston and walk back over the canal bridge, crossing the road. Access to the towpath is on the left. On reaching the water's edge turn right.

Braunston Turn to Braunston Tunnel West Portal - 1¹⁄₂ miles

Strictly speaking, this is the Oxford Canal - see Walk 1 - and before the line was straightened, boats towards Birmingham would have travelled in the direction of the walk. Now they move in the opposite direction. The reason for all this confusion can be seen if you walk back beyond The Boatman for a few yards. There, a couple of very elegant cast iron bridges span the new junction. Ahead is the northern Oxford towards Coventry, whilst the left turn is the new length towards Warwick. The term "new" is relative: it was cut over 180 years ago. Half a mile down the new cut is where the old Oxford turned south through a series of convolutions and even a short tunnel before reaching Braunston.

The original part of this can be found a little way into the proper walking direction. Another cast iron bridge spans the entrance to a large marina. This was the old main line. The building alongside the old junction was the toll house and is now used by British Waterways as an office and visitor centre. There was once a stop lock outside the door. This device lowered the Grand Junction canal into the Oxford, falling only a few inches. It ensured that any boat arriving on the Oxford delivered a small head of water, rather than taking any, and forced the boatmen to stop, thus allowing their boats to be gauged for toll purposes. It was removed during the modernisation, and meant that the level from here to Braunston bottom lock was reduced slightly, albeit not enough to affect boats' movement.

There are several venerable buildings to be found inside the marina, as the Oxford company used it as a warehouse and dry dock area. The extensive lagoon moorings beyond, which continue almost to the lock, were once used as a reservoir by the Oxford.

On the towpath side is a hire company with a boatbuilders to the left. One unusual aspect of operations here is that it is one of the places where the latest canal fad for boats built in the style of Dutch barges is met. The old covered slipway has seen many a new boat

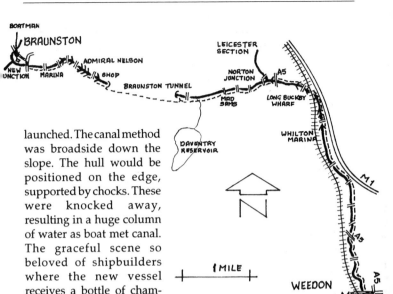

launched. The canal method
was broadside down the
slope. The hull would be
positioned on the edge,
supported by chocks. These
were knocked away,
resulting in a huge column
of water as boat met canal.
The graceful scene so
beloved of shipbuilders
where the new vessel
receives a bottle of cham-
pagne over the bows before
gliding serenely into the water is far removed from the altogether
more earthy approach of canal boatbuilders.

Another dry dock is located alongside the bottom lock on the far
side, and there is a shop on the towpath side. The flight of six locks
is pleasant, punctuated by the occasional old canal house on the far
bank, and the Admiral Nelson pub alongside lock 3. A recently
opened shop selling basic drinks and goodies is located at the top
lock, and from there the canal enters a cutting as it approaches the
tunnel.

Braunston Tunnel West Portal to Buckby Top Lock - 3 miles

There is no towpath through the tunnel, and the newly constructed
path on the right leads away from the canal for a few yards before
turning left. It is difficult to reach the actual tunnel entrance. The
path is well signposted and follows pretty well the course of the
canal underground. There are a couple of brick ventilation shafts
that can be seen en route.

19

Regaining the water's edge beyond, access to the tunnel mouth is possible here. You can peer into the gloom and faintly see the other end. If there are boats on the move lights will shine as they approach. The tunnel itself is just over 2,000 yards long, and two centuries old. There is a pronounced S bend towards the eastern end where the tunnelling gangs did not quite meet. It stood for 180 years before partial failure of the roof lining in the 1970s resulted in an extended closure whilst it was made safe again. The path continues somewhat above water level for $1/4$ mile until the next road bridge at Welton Wharf. A few boats will be discovered tied up across the water, often, again, an old working pair.

This is the short summit of the Grand Junction Canal, and the feeder from Daventry reservoir enters the canal about 300 yards further along. The rolling Northamptonshire hills come steadily into view as the canal leaves its cutting and passes Mad Sams Bridge on the approach to Norton Junction. Across the way, between the main line and the Leicester Section which leaves to the left, is a tiny toll house, delightfully converted into a home. Somewhat shaded from the sun with an easterly aspect, it must be Nirvana for boating enthusiasts.

The Leicester Section - featured in Walks 3 and 4 - was never modernised, and can still only be used by 7ft beam boats. There are many moored craft here as the canal reaches Long Buckby Wharf, the top lock, and the New Inn.

Buckby Top Lock to Whilton Bottom Lock - $1^{1}/_{2}$ miles

The towpath changes sides here, moving to the left bank. Crossing the busy A5 with its high speed traffic was always a problem. Whilst boat crews were ever left to fend for themselves, the introduction of the London to Birmingham walk would greatly increase pedestrian numbers, and a solution was required. A subway was the answer; one that would result in a great deal of egg on the corporate face of British Waterways. Opened in a flurry of publicity, it was christened The People Pipe, and was a godsend. Until it rained. It was then discovered that water ran into the tunnel and the drains were too high to take it away. The resultant - almost continually flooded - pipe was abandoned by walkers who continued to dice with death on the road above. An expensive series of modifications was subsequently made, and the "Pipe" now functions more or less in the manner it was intended.

After another lock, a further refreshment stop is met and beyond, mayhem. The peaceful canal passage has been shattered by the meeting of the London to Glasgow electric railway and the M1 motorway. This narrow corridor created in the upper reaches of the Nene valley carries all three forms of transport very close together, with the old trunk road, the A5, only a few hundred yards to the west. The railway crosses overhead as the canal continues to drop away through more locks.

Whilton Bottom Lock to Weedon - 3 miles

There is another marina behind the bottom lock with offices, and a shop that sells drinks, crisps and ice cream. This somewhat noisy length of the walk continues until the edge of Brockhall Park is reached. Then, by bridge 19, the canal makes a sharp right turn and leaves the motorway behind. This rapidly returns peace to this pretty section of water, as the railway has also moved back to a respectful distance.

Trees give way to pleasant pastureland, broken only briefly by the A5 passing overhead. The course of the canal becomes increasingly twisted as it hugs the contour approaching Weedon. Indeed, it does this so successfully that it will be another 11 miles before the next lock is reached, although there is another - 3,000 yard long - tunnel between. A petrol station to the left of the towpath heralds the approach to Weedon, and around the corner is bridge 24, the end of the walk.

As there was canal interest a few yards beyond the start of this, so there is interest beyond the end. Weedon is the furthest point in England from the coast, and it was here that Weedon Barracks were built. Started in 1803, they contained a Royal Pavilion, to be used by King George III in the event of an invasion by Napoleon. Locals believe it was also to be a staging post during the Second World War. Provisions were made for the (then) Princess Elizabeth and her sister Margaret to be brought here in the event of an invasion. Then, if it were deemed necessary, the girls would be taken to Prestwick airport in Scotland and flown to Canada.

There were extensive buildings, some of which still remain. It was also served by water; the hire boat base a little way along the canal was the start of the arm. It was extant until the 1960s when it was severed as railway electrification arrived.

WALK 3 - MARKET HARBOROUGH TO FOXTON - GRAND UNION CANAL

One of the many short canal branches that tend to be ignored by boaters and walkers alike is the Market Harborough Arm. Why? It's attractive, quiet, and leads to a particularly pleasant basin with lots of canal interest and history. And at the other end is a bonus: Foxton. This famous location of staircase locks and inclined plane offers even more rewarding investigation.

The Market Harborough Arm, opened in 1809, almost seems to have been built to fill in the time whilst the main line from Leicester to Norton Junction, near Braunston, was being talked about and eventually constructed. The original scheme was a canal from Leicester to Northampton with the northern section from Leicester to Debdale actually being built - see Walk 4. Then, with the announcement that the the Grand Junction planned a Northampton Branch, the idea was dropped in favour of a direct link to the Grand Junction at Norton Junction - visited during Walk 2. Work to join the disparate parts was started again in 1810, and the intervening 25 miles were ready by 1814, but at a price. The 17 locks had been built to narrow gauge, and the prospect, long dear to the Grand Junction corporate heart, of a barge canal from London to Yorkshire was stillborn.

Over the intervening years several plans were forwarded to widen this section, the most recent being after the amalgamation of canals that formed the Grand Union in 1928. An application for government money was made, but refused. From then on it was all downhill. Proposals were made for closure in the 1950s, but a vigorous campaign saw the line designated as a cruising canal in the 1968 Act.

Although fairly late to connect with the main system, Market Harborough Basin hosted the seminal Rally in August 1950, when a still virtually ignored and unknown Inland Waterways Association organised the event. Attended by 100 boats, this gathering did much to bring the Inland Waterways Association and its aims to a largely ignorant nation, and showed the world at large the enormous potential for pleasure boating. It would not be too great an exaggeration to say that the use of inland waterways for recreation, as opposed to trade, took off from this event: the seed-corn of today's leisure harvest.

BEFORE YOU START

WALK DISTANCE:	6$^{1}/_{2}$ miles
MAP:	OS Landranger Sheet 141
START:	Car park south-west of Foxton village, created for visitors to the locks
PUBLIC TRANSPORT:	National Coaches and trains to Market Harborough, local bus beyond
STARTING GRID REF:	SP 692892
CAR PARKING:	Pay and display
TRANSPORT:	X62 to Market Harborough. Service details on 01858 462649
REFRESHMENT:	Facilities at each end, little between
NEAREST TIC:	Pen Lloyd Library, Adam and Eve Street, Market Harborough, Leicestershire LE16 7LT - 01858 468106

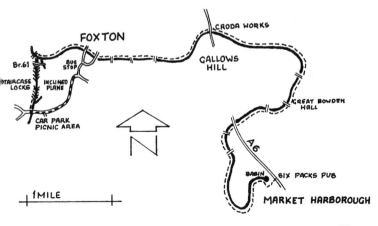

23

THE WALK

Leave the car park, turn right and walk towards Foxton village. At
he junction turn left and after a few yards the Black Horse pub is on
he left. The unmarked bus stop is opposite in the lay-by. Alight at
The Six Packs, on the outskirts of Market Harborough.

Market Harborough to Gallows Hill Bridge - 3¹/₂ miles

Cross the road and to the left-hand side of the pub is a track that will
take you into the basin. Note a sign alongside the pub informing that
they have a restuarant (*sic*). This unusual name marks the six packs
of foxhounds in the county. The Pychley, The Ferney and the world
famous Quorn all meet in this area. Whatever your views on this
alleged sport the sight of hounds in full cry followed by a crowd of
suicide-seeking horse riders is very exciting. Its original name was
The Union Inn, but it was changed to avoid confusion with the
Union Warehouse across the road. The basin is home to Harborough
Marine, and Anglo Welsh Cruisers, two very well known canal
names associated with boatbuilding and boat hire respectively.
Follow a track behind the buildings to the left and turn right
beyond. This returns to the towpath at the neck of the basin. Usually
empty of visiting boats, it is an area of great tranquillity.

Only ¹/₂ mile into this walk the canal makes a 180 degree turn to
head generally north, and the rolling countryside of Leicestershire
unfolds. The course of the canal for the first 2 miles is extremely
convoluted, matching anything James Brindley produced on the
Oxford Canal - see Walk 1. A mile further, the second crossing is a
turnover bridge taking the towpath to the right-hand side of the
water where it will remain until just before the end of this walk.
After the noisy A6 passes overhead, the towpath moves away to
relative solitude again with not a lot of canal infrastructure to vary
the diet of delightful views and peaceful plodding.

Great Bowden Hall backs to the canal at bridge 10, followed by
some rather up-market housing in grounds that once belonged to
the hall. The towpath quality deteriorates markedly from this point
until the outskirts of Foxton village, but after the next bridge the
water makes a broad left sweep as it hangs to the contour, and gives
stunning views over this pretty county with Langton Hall visible
across on the far hillside.

Industry rears its ugly head after another mile as a tall chimney belonging to Croda Processed Chemicals comes into view. The works backs to the canal, and the A6 again passes overhead.

Gallows Hill Bridge to Foxton - 3 miles

That really is the last of the intrusions to the peace of this canal. Look in the fields to the right beyond this bridge. Remains of the medieval ridge and furrow method of agriculture are clear to see.

The canal straightens its course now as it reaches the outskirts of Foxton. There are three bridges in fairly quick succession before a swing bridge is discovered, the only one on this line. Hard by the next bridge, the Black Horse pub (where the bus stop is located) offers the chance of refreshment. An even more interesting pub lies at the junction, just $^1/_2$ mile further.

Bear to the right with the towpath, cross the first bridge and turn left towards the locks. Here, across the bridge by the bottom chamber, is Bridge 61 - that is the name of the pub as well as its location, a free house at the heart of things on the junction. That, and an interesting little shop next door, are all mixed in with the Foxton Boat Services empire creating a delightfully untidy panorama. The pub has an extremely good range of quality beers on offer, and the temptation to linger longer is strong.

But there is still much to see. Ahead, the ten chambers of Foxton locks climb the hill, arranged in two sets of five with side ponds and a passing space. A description of the workings will be found in Walk 17. These were the original locks that were to be superseded by the inclined plane. The few remains of this incredible structure are over to the left. Opened in 1900 the high operating cost and relative lack of boats meant that it was hopelessly expensive to operate, and only had a very short life, closing in 1911. There were two huge tanks, one at the top, the other at the bottom. Boats would be pulled into these, doors closed, and water-filled caisson and boat hauled to the other level. There the door was opened and the boat continued on the new level.

All the machinery was dismantled and sold, but the earthworks, separate canal cuts and engine house remain, the latter converted into a museum showing, with models and old photographs, how things were. Lots of restoration work has been carried out by a trust dedicated to preserving the site, and there is much to explore. One wonderful link with the past is that the rails on which the caissons travelled were bought from the old Great Western Railway. They were once part of their 7ft gauge track: from Brunel to Foxton, and still extant.

When you have finally had your fill of this superb area, the walk continues up the flight. At the top pause awhile and admire the surrounding countryside. And envy the site of the lock keeper's cottage, high on the hill with panoramic views that must be one of the best canalside locations in the country. A short distance beyond, the towpath meets a bridge. Leave the canal, turn left, and the car park is a little further along on the right.

WALK 4 - LEICESTER TO SOUTH WIGSTON - GRAND UNION CANAL AND RIVER SOAR

A walk that manages to produce that strange "canal effect" when walking through an urban area. Despite the noise and mayhem around, the canal manages to stay peaceful and serene.

To give this canal its Sunday name, it is the Leicester Arm of the Grand Union Canal. The River Soar to Leicester was made navigable in 1794 and the Grand Junction (forerunner of the Grand Union) was building from London to Braunston. A link between the river and Northampton was considered a good idea. An Act for a wide beamed canal was obtained and construction was soon under way. The rest of this tale is told in Walk 3.

BEFORE YOU START

WALK DISTANCE:	7 Miles
MAP:	OS Landranger Series No 140
START:	Crow Mill Bridge, South Wigston. This is on a secondary road 3 miles south-east of junction 21, M1. Take Blaby Road from Blaby in the direction of Wigston and turn right following the Countesthorpe road
PUBLIC TRANSPORT:	Excellent service to Leicester
STARTING GRID REF:	SP 588977

Roman remains in Leicester

CAR PARKING:	Large park adjacent
TRANSPORT:	Midland Fox service to the centre of Leicester. A more frequent service - number 48 - operates from Blaby Road near the junction and a walk back to there is often the best move. Service details on 01533 511411
REFRESHMENT:	Nothing at the start. Everything - and more - in Leicester. One pub en route
NEAREST TIC:	7-9 Every Street, Town Hall Square, Leicester, Leicestershire LE1 6AG - 0116 265 0555

THE WALK

Alight outside the Holiday Inn on St. Nicholas Circle. The walk will start at West Bridge which, unsurprisingly, is to the west of the bus stop. But before setting forth spend a few moments in this, the oldest area in Leicester.

Castle Park was first settled by the Romans. *Ratae Corieltauvorum* was originally a military crossing point over the Soar. Subsequently, civilians followed and built housing. A section of their work is still extant. Jewry Wall dates from AD 150 and is the largest surviving Roman civilian building in England. It was probably the wall of an exercise hall. Although not on the normal route of seekers after Roman antiquities, Leicester is one of the oldest remaining settlements, and certainly pre-dates more illustrious sites in York and London.

Predictably, there is little evidence of the town during the centuries after the Romans left our shores. People lived there: that's for sure. There was a bishopric established during the eighth century, but that lapsed, not to be revived until 1919. Indeed, the next real record comes from Domesday. There were six churches and 322 houses recorded in that priceless census. The Normans moved into town and the place developed slowly, if undramatically until the Industrial Revolution. Again, this riverside area was where businesses were sited. Hosiery and footwear manufacture were the staple trades, as they are today. This is now augmented by engineering, a relatively new arrival but again sited by the river.

St. Nicholas' Church is the oldest in Leicester and can be seen here. Some of the original Saxon work was included in the largely

Norman rebuilding.

West Bridge to Kings Lock - 4 miles

St. Augustine Road leads to West Bridge. There are six crossings over the river, this one being the first. West Gate was located here but was dismantled long ago. The current iron bridge was built in 1890. Cross the water and on the right-hand side is a flight of steps down to the water. Turn right, back under the bridge.

Hard by this point is an arch featuring bas-relief mermaids. It came from the Rutland Street entrance to Humberstone Gate Vegetable Market (1902) when that building was demolished in 1972. The figures came from the Doulton Pottery in Lambeth, London. They were erected here in 1982 on the site of a pillar that supported the Great Central Railway as it crossed the water. This company was the penultimate transmogrification of a group of railways that finally opened a line to London in the very early days of the twentieth century. It had development from The Leicester and Swannington Railway whose terminus was close by. Opened in 1832 it was one of the earliest railways in the country. Conceived as a coal-carrying enterprise it subsequently developed a rudimentary passenger service. The

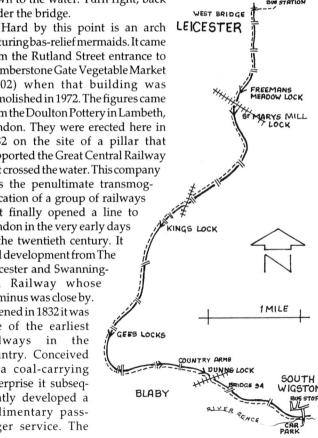

BUS STATION

WEST BRIDGE

LEICESTER

FREEMANS MEADOW LOCK

St MARYS MILL LOCK

KINGS LOCK

N

1 MILE

GEES LOCKS

COUNTRY ARMS

DUNNS LOCK

BRIDGE 94

BLABY

SOUTH WIGSTON

BUS STOP

RIVER SENCE

CAR PARK

Great Central Railway reached here in 1899. This was a development of the Manchester, Sheffield and Lincolnshire Railway and the link to London Marylebone was intended as competition for the Midland from Sheffield, Nottingham and Leicester, and the London and North Western Railway from Manchester and Rugby. There was a link to the Great Western between Woodford Halse and Banbury that is passed during Walk 1. It became a victim of BR cuts. Having decided that the midland route was preferable, services were reduced, slow and inconveniently timed. The line was finally closed in 1969.

This section of river is known as the Straight Mile, for obvious reasons. It was built in 1890 as part of the Leicester Corporation flood prevention measures. An annual rowing regatta is held here, which is very popular with the locals. The towpath crosses a very ornate iron bridge towards the end of the straight. At this point Freemans Meadow lock is reached.

Beyond, another iron bridge takes the walk over one of the many backwaters that weave their way around this, the Soar valley. The walk is currently a mixture of canalised and natural river, and continues as such for some distance yet. At St. Marys Mill lock there are seats and an information board.

In fact these are repeated at most locks on the river section. The towpath is of excellent quality being either metalled or well packed, weed-free earth, right back to South Wigston. Aylestone Nature Reserve is on the right during this section and, prosaically, the gasworks is across on the left. Around the next bend there is a gasholder on the right as well but this aberration is short-lived.

Pass under the ex-Great Central Railway bridge and the River Soar is crossed again. This time it leaves for good. Beyond is Kings lock and the first real canal. It is also the finish of the area adopted by the council for full recreational treatment. Seats, signposts and information boards are all part of this manifestation, the whole area being known as Riverside Park.

Kings Lock to Crow Mill Bridge - 3 miles

After Kings Lock what was clearly a canalised river is now equally clearly a pure canal. The edging is piled and shrubs that grew along the water's edge are now no more. The scenery remains pretty with a slight urban feel as successive locks and bridges are passed. So far the walk has headed generally south, but this is about to change. A sharp left-hand bend makes the new heading easterly as yet another ex-Great Central Railway overbridge appears. At bridge 98 there is a pub/restaurant on the right, the Country Arms. Although unattractive from the outside, the pub has excellent food, the beer is very palatable, and the ambience inside first class.

Housing starts to make its presence felt on the far bank, a suburban development, with pretty gardens that run right to the water's edge. Bridge 95 is completely new and more housing follows on the right. Bridge 94 carries the usual cast iron plate proclaiming it to be Little Glen Bridge 94, but also has the number cast as a concrete keystone, together with the construction date: 1923.

Just before Crow Mill Bridge turn right into the car park, also built on the site of an old railway, this time the old London and North Western Railway Leicester to Rugby line.

WALK 5 - NORTHAMPTON TO BLISWORTH - GRAND UNION CANAL

Northamptonshire really is a pretty county, and this walk shows it off to advantage with continuous dramatic contrasts. A rural backwater, Blisworth is now thankfully free of the A43 trunk road which used to thunder through it. Busy motorways and the city of Northampton are counterpointed by bucolic settings that are absolutely timeless. A look at the history of the Grand Union will be found in Walk 2.

BEFORE YOU START

WALK DISTANCE:	6 miles
MAP:	OS Landranger Sheet 152
START:	The canal bridge in Blisworth. The village is east of the Northampton to Towcester road near junction 15A on the M1
PUBLIC TRANSPORT:	Northampton is nearest
STARTING GRID REF:	SP 724535

CAR PARKING:	Side streets
TRANSPORT:	Stagecoach United Counties services 38 and X38 into Northampton. Only the latter one operates on Sundays. Details on 01604 20077
REFRESHMENT:	Start and finish only
NEAREST TIC:	Visitor Centre, Mr. Grant's House, 10 St. Giles Square, Northampton, Northants NN1 1DA - 01604 22677

THE WALK

A few moments spent around the village admiring thatched cottages and the church is time well spent. The bus stop is outside the church. Alight at the New Bridge on the Towcester road near the Kentucky Fried Chicken building. Walk back over the bridge and you will see a path down to the canal. Northampton lock, where the canal joins the River Nene, is a few yards to your left, but the walk turns right, away from the town.

Northampton to Hardingstone Lock - 1½ miles

Beyond the lock is the home of Carlsberg lager, built on the site of the old Phipps brewery. The locks on this Northampton Arm are narrow (7ft) ones, quite a culture shock for boats approaching from either end. These seem quite intimate after the broad beam caverns on both the Nene and Grand Union main line.

The river, canal and a railway line run parallel for some distance before another noisy electric railway crosses overhead. This is not the most pleasant part of town, but is very soon left behind as the scenery rapidly becomes quite rural. A somewhat muddy towpath at the start is soon replaced by a firm grassy way that is not overused by the locals. The canal then runs through peaceful water meadows with the river never too far away until Hardingstone lock is reached.

Hardingstone Lock to M1 Motorway - 1½ miles

Beyond this lock the Nene waves its farewell and departs westward as the canal turns south. But, appearing unwilling to leave the canal alone, a small tributary stays with it for about ½ a mile before passing under the line in a culvert.

Banbury (Walk 1)

Market Harborough basin, Grand Union Leicester branch (Walk 3)

Marson Junction, where the Ashby and Coventry canals meet (Walk 6)

Awsworth Viaduct (Walk 8)

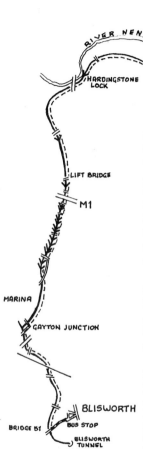

NØRTHAMPTON

1 MILE

Although this is pretty countryside, aural pollution starts to become evident and the character of the canal will undergo something of a metamorphosis. Ahead is a new brick bridge, part of a large road improvement scheme in the area. This carries the new A43 Oxford to Northampton road that used to pass through Blisworth. Once there was a railway line here but the new road has taken much of its course.

To allow access to and from the M1 a new junction - 15A - has been created at Rothersthorpe service area. However, compare the pretty rustic brick bridges that carry the new roads with the gaunt concrete cavern that is the M1.

M1 Motorway to Gayton Junction - 2 miles

The locks have now started in earnest. Just before the motorway is an original lift bridge constructed in the old style and hauled up by chain. The remains of one of these lies in ruins by lock 11 but the one by lock 5 is intact. The new road is just over the boundary on the left, delaying the return to peaceful surroundings for a while. All too soon the locks are over. A very attractive lock keeper's cottage with tile hung walls and a simply magnificent location signifies the top of the flight. Behind, the broad expanse of the Nene valley is laid out.

The large marina and hire boat base a few yards along provides a spectacle of boats. These are not too common on the Northampton arm generally. Alvechurch Boat Company operates a hire fleet from here which makes it a very busy location on summer Saturdays. There is also a large collection of privately owned boats to ensure that variety is never missing.

On reaching the roving bridge number 2, instead of crossing the canal it is a wise move to vacate the towpath and follow the road to the left as far as the main line where a left turn is made. Sticking to the waterside the towpath will turn right at the junction and depart in the opposite direction. Then it is necessary to walk about 300 yards in the wrong direction before another roving bridge takes the towpath over the water and allows a left turn. British Waterways have a yard here, and the house set on the junction is called the Old Toll House - for obvious reasons.

Gayton Junction to Blisworth - 1 mile

Walking south now, the electric railway again makes a noisy appearance overhead, followed by the new road. Attractive canalside houses announce your arrival in Blisworth. Blisworth Tunnel Boats and moored craft on either side of the towpath make this a thoroughly interesting area, and there are boats on the move here even in the depths of winter.

The walk ends by the mill at bridge 51, but if you are feeling energetic the entrance to the longest currently navigable tunnel in England is only another 300 yards away. From there you can peer into the Stygian gloom and watch for the lights of approaching boats. It's quite amazing how long they will take to reach the tunnel mouth.

For refreshment there is a very nice pub in the centre on the village. Then, whilst you are in the area, it's only a short drive into Stoke Bruerne, home of British Waterways' Waterway Museum. It's well worth the detour, and the road you take runs directly over Blisworth tunnel, as you can see from the ventilation shafts. There's a wealth of interest in the museum itself, and the whole area is one of tremendous canal interest.

Ancient lift bridge on the Northampton Arm

WALK 6 - SHENTON TO SHACKERSTONE - ASHBY CANAL

Lock free, and almost entirely bucolic, this walk has not a lot of variety to offer the committed canal enthusiast. But with a vintage steam railway and one of the most important historic battlefields to be found in England, there is much to intrigue and fascinate the walker. Transport, though, is a major problem.

The steam railway, on which the walk depends, operates at weekends only from March to October - with a few "Santa Specials" around Christmas, and a Wednesday service in high season. *Be careful to check operating details before planning this walk.* A look at the history of the Ashby Canal will be found in Walk 21.

BEFORE YOU START

WALK DISTANCE:	5½ miles
MAP:	OS Landranger Series No 140
START:	Shackerstone station on The Battlefield Line, a steam railway. The village is to the east of the A444 at Twycross, 4 miles south of its intersection with the M42. Twycross Zoo is well signed; the railway less so
PUBLIC TRANSPORT:	Non-existent. Tamworth is the nearest point
STARTING GRID REF:	SK 379066
CAR PARKING:	Large park provided by the railway a short distance to the north of the station. Follow the signs
TRANSPORT:	Limited. The steam railway operates as mentioned above. Full details on 01827 880754
REFRESHMENT:	Nothing save what can be found on the railway
NEAREST TIC:	Bosworth Battlefield Visitor Centre, Sutton Cheney, Market Bosworth, Leicestershire CV13 0AD - 01455 292239

THE WALK

Catch the train to Shenton and alight there. This is a very popular

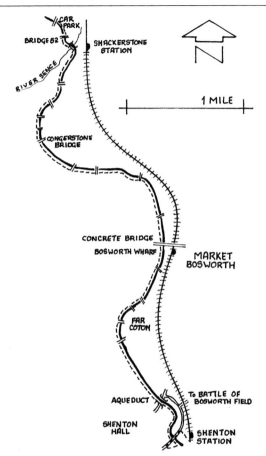

spot for visitors, being so close to the site where the English crown was won - and lost - on an English battlefield for the very last time: Bosworth Field. The ticket office on the far platform was originally built at Humberstone Road Station, Leicester. A listed building, it was creating a headache when a road widening scheme was mooted around its original site.

The Battlefield Line solved the problem. They wanted a building and here was one going begging. It was carefully demolished in December 1992, every item being marked, and transported here. Foundations were laid during September 1993 and the place re-erected, each brick in the correct place. British Rail provided most of the funding for this careful and time-consuming exercise. The building that now graces the platform shows it as money well spent.

Shenton Station to Bridge 42 to Market Bosworth - 2 miles

Leave Shenton station through the car park and turn left up the road towards the canal. To gain the towpath it is necessary to cross the bridge and walk on for some 30 yards before a signpost indicates the way back. At the water's edge turn left, under the bridge.

The towpath here is in good condition, and will remain so for virtually all the walk. This first section is very heavily used by strollers drawn to the Battlefield Centre. The actual centre is quite a way from the canal, and possibly best left until after the walk. There are walks throughout the area of the conflict, and interpretation boards are well located all around. Following these through the course of events is to tread the footsteps of history.

It was 22 August 1485 when Richard III lost the crown to Henry Tudor on Ambion Hill. Richard died in the thick of the battle, the victim of a disastrous succession of conspiracies that within a short space of time claimed the lives of all the male heirs to the house of York. For Henry, the battle was the last in a whirlwind series of events that propelled him from penniless exile in 1483 to King Henry VII just two years later.

The sequence of events and machinations leading to Bosworth are chronicled in many learned tomes, and the dramatisation by Shakespeare is far more relevant and comprehensible after a visit to the field. We have no way of knowing for certain whether Richard really did offer his kingdom for a horse, but, even with all the wonders of modern communications, we cannot get history correct today; witness the varying accounts and interpretations of the Falklands and Gulf wars.

As with virtually every other town and village on this canal, Shenton is set well away from the water. This intriguing village, visible on the left, centres round the Hall, parts of which date back to 1629. The road leading there is crossed by the canal on a brick

Attractive rural scenery on the Ashby Canal

aqueduct. Around here the canal has been improved on the opposite bank to provide moorings for boats visiting The Battlefield Centre.

In lonely splendour the line wriggles its way north, crossed only by a couple of pretty brick bridges. Then moored boats, a much more modern bridge, and, heaven forfend, human activity. This is Market Bosworth Wharf, once the freight centre of the town, a mile to the east. Now it has been made thoroughly attractive - in particular the bridge, a low modern one to carry heavy traffic on a secondary road. Flower troughs have been provided and, in summer at least, the whole area presents a bright cheerful face to the outside world.

Market Bosworth Wharf to Shackerstone Station - 3½ miles

More brick bridges follow in rapid succession. For reasons best known to themselves their traffic load varies between very little and nothing, so the remoteness factor is undisturbed. Only anglers and an occasional boat offer the chance to speak to another human.

Congerstone is approached, but at the last moment, when contact with the village seems inevitable, the line turns sharp right and runs away into the last section of the walk. More moored boats are discovered as signs of railway activity can be seen to the right. A further aqueduct over the River Sence and a left turn brings bridge 52 into view. This is the end of the walk, and a roving bridge to boot.

Turn right over the water and down the road to the car park. To reach the station take the first on the right and a drive leads to the station buildings. It also offers the chance to make a closer examination of the aqueduct, being right alongside the drive. Whilst there, consider the road bridge as well; it's a Grade II listed cast iron structure.

The railway has a fascinating museum for those interested in that kind of thing. It houses what is recognised as one of the most interesting collections in the country, with many items dating back to the last century. The station itself was opened in 1873, and was the headquarters of the Ashby and Nuneaton Joint Railway. This was absorbed into the Midland Railway, who eventually bought the canal.

A few yards beyond the end of the walk is Gopsall Wharf. This was the last canalside location on the Ashby to load Leicestershire coal into narrowboats. This was despatched down the canal, along the Coventry, Oxford and Grand Union canals, where it eventually reached Hertfordshire papermakers. The trade finally died in the early 1980s and the coal is no longer mined.

WALK 7 - OUNDLE CIRCULAR - RIVER NENE

Within the meaning of the Act, this is not truly a canal walk. However the sylvan waters of the navigable River Nene, a couple of (very short) canalised sections, extensive water meadows and lakes fully justify its place within these covers.

Being a river, the history of navigation is long. The earliest record of attempts to improve the river are to be found in ecclesiastical documents from around 1500. That saw the construction of a navigable channel to improve drainage and linked Peterborough with the Wash. Successive piecemeal improvements continued over the next two centuries. Oundle was reached in 1730, and Northampton in 1761. There were eventually 38 locks between that town and the open sea.

Trade was never heavy, even after the Grand Junction's Northampton Arm connected in 1815 - see Walk 5, P31. The locks had fallen into disrepair by the end of the nineteenth century. In the 1930s an ambitious scheme to improve the whole river was undertaken. Primarily flood control measures, the unusual guillotine locks were built at this time. Now it is a popular boating river with no commercial traffic.

BEFORE YOU START

WALK DISTANCE:	5 miles
MAP:	OS Landranger Series No 141
START:	Barnwell Visitor Centre, Barnwell Road, Oundle. This lies to the south of the A427, signposted on along a minor road from the town
PUBLIC TRANSPORT:	Limited. Kettering and Peterborough are the nearest large towns with any reasonable service
STARTING GRID REF:	TL 037871
CAR PARKING:	On the site
REFRESHMENT:	Pub soon after the start, the nothing until Oundle. Plenty there
NEAREST TIC:	14 West Street, Oundle, Northants PE8 4EF - 01832 274333

Barnwell Park to Ashton Lock - 2½ miles

Leave the car park heading towards a lake, away from Oundle but keeping close to the road. This path comes tight alongside a lake and then closes on a fence to the left as the river lock comes into view. At the end of the fence a gap gives access to a drive which leads to a road. Turn right, cross the road and river, where access to the towpath will be found, signposted as The Nene Way. A few yards beyond this turn, hard by the lock, is a free house called The Mill. Whilst not directly on the walk it's a super place to call for a break - after 300 yards' walking!

The Nene Way, Irchester to Wansford section was opened by the

The Mill pub by Upper Barnwell Lock on the River Nene

Duke of Gloucester on 5 April 1990. Today it gives a splendid long distance walk along most of the river. The path is wide and very well surfaced and leads after a short distance to Lower Barnwell lock. The oddity that is a Nene lock can be studied in detail. The top gates are standard mitre pattern but the bottom ones are a huge guillotine gate. These act as a clough to release the water and are laboriously wound high enough to admit boats. This used to be a very long and tiring job as the gearing was so low. Today the trend is to power the mechanism so that what was once over a hundred turns on a windlass becomes a long press on a button.

At this chamber the path crosses a footbridge attached to the lower gate and leads directly away from the water. Follow this over two footbridges which cross small offshoots of the river and walk to the fence across a field. On reaching this the path turns almost back on itself to regain the edge of the main river only some 100 yards further down. The guide for this angle is a willow tree that has seen better days. Why this apparent anomaly in a right of way should exist is one of those idiosyncrasies that infuriate and delight at the same time.

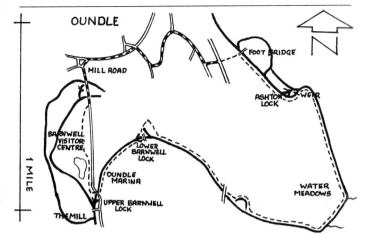

Pass under a road bridge which strides out over the flood plain and follow the course of the river as it describes a huge arc, avoiding Oundle at all costs. The scenery stays uniformly beautiful as meadow succeeds meadow until Ashton lock is reached.

Ashton Lock to Barnwell Park - 2½ miles

A slight diversion from the water's edge here as the path turns left to a stile before a right turn regains the river. Delightfully bucolic views continue until a footbridge is reached. Here, the Nene Way crosses to the right but the walk turns left towards the road. Cross, and follow the Public Footpath sign to the end of this lane. Turn right and follow this to the junction. Turn left into East Road, right at the end, and at the top, left. This now gives a chance to explore this pretty little town.

There is a foodstore, a pub the Angel - John Smiths - and several other establishments in the town. Pass the TIC and follow the road to the far end. Here, at a fork with an octagonal tower and a cruciform building, bear left and first left again into Mill Road. Cross a very attractive stone bridge which leads to an entrance into Barnwell Country Park. Take this and follow the water's edge back to the car park. At this point it is possible to extend the walk by almost a mile. Turn right and follow the clearly defined path around the country park.

Chapter 2:
Nottinghamshire and Derbyshire

WALK 8 - ILKESTON CIRCULAR - EREWASH & NOTTINGHAM CANALS

Whilst this walk fits the "canalside walk" category, it is not entirely alongside water. Two linking roads and some infilled canal line are included in this circular excursion.

The Erewash ran from the River Trent northwards and climbed 109ft to Langley Mill, generally along the west side of the Erewash valley. It was a profitable canal for its owners and, unlike the competition, never came into railway ownership. It was eventually absorbed into the Grand Union Canal system in 1932. Carrying finished in 1952 and the upper section above Gallows lock was officially abandoned in 1962. However, the need to maintain a water supply channel meant that it was not totally neglected, and several years later, when the potential for leisure use was perceived, the two local councils were able to work with British Waterways for restoration to cruising standard. Now complete its future is secure.

Which can also now be said of what remains of the Nottingham Canal. This ran 14 miles from that city and the River Trent to Langley Mill where it also met the Cromford Canal in Great Northern Basin. Although this was competition for the Erewash it also brought a general increase in trade to the area. The Nottingham cost £80,000 to construct and was engineered by William Jessop. It opened in 1796 and carried mainly coal, augmented by iron products from the Butterley Company. There were good profits for its proprietors for many years until falling traffic forced a sale to the railways in 1855.

Trade died slowly, with the lower reaches still just in use by the 1920s. By 1928 the last cargo had moved. The northern reaches of the Nottingham Canal were abandoned in 1937, although the section from Lenton to the Trent through the city centre is still in use today.

En route this canal passed the edge of Eastwood, the birthplace

Gallows Lock on the Erewash Canal

of D.H. Lawrence. Needless to say, the town is particularly proud of its most famous son, and much is made of the fact locally. Part of his *Sons and Lovers* is actually set in the town. Those of a literary bent would do well to visit the town after finishing this walk, if only to visit the splendid museum devoted to the author.

Along with the Thames and Severn Canal, the Nottingham holds a place in literature, being mentioned extensively in Lawrence's book *The Rainbow*. Set in the village of Cossall, close by the canal, he wrote, "...the canal embankment, which rose like a high rampart near at hand, so that occasionally a man's figure passed in silhouette, or a man and a towing horse traversed the sky". Further into the book, we read, "Then, a short time afterwards, a colliery was sunk on the other side of the canal, and in a while the Midland Railway came down the valley at the foot of the Ilkeston hill".

For the record, the Thames and Severn Canal was featured in one of C.S. Forrester's Hornblower novels. There is a fine and generally accurate description of a fly-boat journey along that canal early in the nineteenth century.

BEFORE YOU START

WALK DISTANCE:	7 miles (shortened version 4 miles)
MAP:	OS Landranger Sheet 129
START:	On the A6096 Ilkeston to Kimberley road
PUBLIC TRANSPORT:	Langley Mill (Regional Railways) is 3 miles to the north (with bus connection). Intercity Nottingham
STARTING GRID REF:	SK 471423
CAR PARKING:	Available on side roads
REFRESHMENT:	Plenty of pubs on the Erewash length, nothing in the Nottingham section. Ilkeston has everything
NEAREST TIC:	1-4 Smithy Row, Nottingham NG1 2BY - 0115 977 3448. Granada Motorway Services Area, M1 Northbound, Nottinghamshire NG9 3PL - 0115 944 2411

Ilkeston to Nottingham Canal - 2 miles

Join the towpath by the steps on the bridge and turn left (south). The towpath is good quality, although the surroundings are a little urban. Green spaces to the right are rapidly followed by more housing, whilst factories crowd a narrow isthmus formed by the canal and railway. This was the section that was abandoned in 1962, but is in good repair now.

Gallows lock is the point to leave the Erewash canal. The Inn takes its name from gallows that once stood here. In the fourteenth century the plague threatened to wipe out the judiciary of Nottingham, so they moved the Assizes to Ilkeston. The execution of condemned criminals took place here until 1870 when the gallows were blown down in a storm. There was a pub on this site before the canal arrived. The first clear record is from 1765, and it had become the Gallows by 1798. The current building dates back to 1936.

Turn left, along the A6007, towards Trowell. After 200 yards the River Erewash is crossed. This is the county line; the walk moves from Derbyshire to Nottinghamshire. By the board announcing this fact is a path to the left which goes over a railway footbridge, and up a bank to the Nottingham Canal. Follow it and turn left on reaching the "canal".

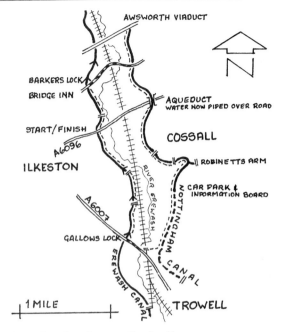

Nottingham Canal to Awsworth - 3 miles

The line here is infilled but after ¹/₄ mile the site of a swing bridge can be clearly seen, the first of several on this length. The masonry is all that remains here. After ¹/₂ mile a car park with large information board heralds water again - just. Thoroughly weed choked and only a few inches deep, it is still a very pleasant walk. Look across the valley. It's amazing how industry and housing has clung to the western slope. Over here it's a different world: green, thoroughly rural, and seemingly miles away from Ilkeston and industry.

Clinging tenaciously to the contour, the canal bears to the right. Over the field to the left is the line of a hedge. That is where we will be in a few minutes as the course swings around almost 180 degrees left, showing all the characteristics of Brindley. But the great man had no hand in this canal; it was engineered by William Jessop. At the head of the turn lies the Robinetts Arm. This short branch served a colliery, and provided water for the main line.

The masonry connected with another swing bridge can be seen next. But pause awhile and examine it. There were flood gates fitted to the side, and the remains of one can still be seen. As the canal has been closed over 50 years, it is interesting to speculate on its age.

The hillside ahead, green and with young trees planted, has not always looked so pretty. Not too many years ago this was a colliery spoil head, one of the many lowered and landscaped after the Aberfan disaster in the 1960s. Beyond it you can look back and see that some of the area has been put to another good use: a first class dry ski slope now adorns the north-west side.

Ahead, the towpath comes to an abrupt end at an aqueduct. The original structure was removed many years ago, and a concrete framework carrying cast iron pipes built in its place. There is an old railway bridge alongside that can be used for crossing the road. Here, you can follow the shortened walk by simply turning left and walking along the main road for $1/2$ mile back to the starting point.

For the more intrepid there is still much to see. The canal continues its convoluted course to the next road bridge. Here the walk will eventually turn left back towards the Erewash. But first there are a further 600 yards to explore. This short section is used by fishermen, and the water is deeper and weed free.

The superb Bennerley (or Awsworth) viaduct, which spans the valley here, once brought the Great Northern Railway into the Nottinghamshire coalfields. This caused much consternation to the local company, the Midland, who saw some of their profits being creamed off. Now long disused, the point where it crosses the canal marks the start of another infilled section that lasts almost to Langley Mill.

Awsworth to Ilkeston - 2 miles

From here return to the road bridge and turn right, down into the valley. As you approach the railway bridge extra care is needed. This road carries a lot of heavy vehicles and there is no footpath on the bridge itself, just a very narrow grass verge on which to escape. After $1/2$ mile the walk reaches the Erewash Canal again at Common Bottom (Barkers) lock. Turn left and a pleasantly quiet towpath awaits - quiet after the road, that is. Very quickly Ilkeston starts to make its presence felt, although there is still a mile of pleasant canalside walking left until the starting point is reached.

WALK 9 - AMBERGATE TO CROMFORD - CROMFORD CANAL

Spectacular Derbyshire scenery and loads of interest - both canal and otherwise - make this a rather special walk.

Opened in 1794 to link with the Erewash Canal - see Walk 8 - the Cromford Canal ran for $14^{1/2}$ miles from the basin in Cromford to Langley Mill. It traded profitably for many years until the through link was severed in 1900 by the collapse of a 3,000 yard long tunnel at Butterley. Some local trade continued until the infamous 1944 Act saw it legally abandoned. Derbyshire County Council took over the remains in 1974 and, despite a series of subsequent problems, the future seems secure.

The old warehouses at Cromford Basin, Cromford Canal

49

Railways were inextricably linked with this canal from very early times. Inconceivable as it may now seem, the original plan was to connect the Cromford with the Upper Peak Forest at Whaley Bridge, high in the Pennines. (This area is explored in *Canal Walks - North*.) The noted engineer James Rennie actually surveyed a route in 1810, but the expense of constructing the line which would have included a tunnel almost 3 miles long saw the idea stillborn. However, a link between this industrially active area and Manchester was still needed: enter the Cromford and High Peak Railway.

The Cromford end of this dramatic railway, with rope operated inclines as steep as 1 in 8 and rising to 1,264ft above sea level, was opened in 1830, and throughout, 14 months later. It was ever a beast of a line to operate with constant problems from the weather, and included the steepest gradient in the country - 1 in 14 - worked by normal adhesion methods. It closed in 1967 and much of its course is now a public footpath, the High Peak Trail. The first incline, a couple of old guards vans, and a Ranger office on Cromford Wharf, where goods were trans-shipped, all help to give a flavour of what once was.

The "other" railway is also of great interest. Once, the Midland Railway's main line from London to Manchester was vibrant with freight and express passenger trains. Opened in 1867 it survived just a century before being closed between Matlock and Chinley, further north. A preservation society is working on an ambitious scheme to restore the link with Buxton which, if they succeed, will make a magnificent addition to our network of preserved railways along such a scenic route.

On this route the first passenger diesel locos of the Modernisation programme in the 1950s were introduced. It also saw a very popular blue painted diesel Pullman service which ran until 1966. Then the electrified Manchester to London via Rugby service was preferred and this line lost almost everything. Today the ubiquitous railcar grumbles its way along the valley calling at every station; a sad reflection of the glory days now gone for ever.

BEFORE YOU START

WALK DISTANCE:	5¹/₂ miles
MAP:	OS Landranger Sheet 119
START:	Cromford Station on the Derby - Matlock Regional Railways line
PUBLIC TRANSPORT:	Intercity to Derby, National Coaches to Matlock
STARTING GRID REF:	SK 303574
CAR PARKING:	At the station
TRANSPORT:	Train to Ambergate. TransPeak bus service R1 operates from Cromford crossroads to Ambergate. Details from 01332 292200
REFRESHMENT:	Matlock Bath has everything, minimal enroute
NEAREST TIC:	The Pavilion, Matlock Bath, Derbyshire DE4 3NR - 01629 55082

THE WALK

Alight at Ambergate railway station, which is just off the A6 Derby to Matlock road. Leave the car park and turn left down a flight of steps to the road, left under the railway bridge and right when you reach the A6. The Hurt Arms is opposite and a Little Chef around the corner. About 150 yards up the road turn right into Chase Road and the canal is a few yards along.

Ambergate to Whatstandwell - 2 miles

The walk turns left, but to the right the water continues for just a few yards. Here an aqueduct over the A610 was demolished as part of a road improvement scheme, leaving the northern reaches of this beautiful canal forever isolated.

Heading north, the first couple of miles are almost devoid of canal infrastructure interest. But the narrow Derwent valley, which holds canal, railway and road between its steep sides, is always pretty, sometimes dramatic. The towpath is rather less well cared for but easily walkable. The first buildings, Canal Cottages, are used by St. John's Ambulance for the expansion of their good work. The towpath is on an embankment here - quite the norm, as will soon be revealed.

51

One of the many beautiful features on the canal are the flowers: rhododendrons, bluebells and flag irises depending on the season. They grow in profusion, adding a scintillating dimension to this walk. English Heritage have listed the whole canal as a Site of Special Scientific Interest, and wildlife flourishes.

Whatstandwell to Cromford Basin - 3¹⁄₂ miles

Just beyond Whatstandwell station is a car park, and from here the towpath improves dramatically and, with it, the number of strollers and dog walkers. A narrow section next, where the cut clings to the hillside in a manner reminiscent of the Llangollen Canal, just before it reaches that town, and every bit as pretty too. Beyond are a few houses clustered together, with carefully manicured lawns reaching down to the water's edge and a private crossing over the water. There are quite a few of these on the walk, which take varying forms from large stepping stones to slippery planks precariously balanced on wobbling masonry.

The next bridge has an Ordnance Survey benchmark in its buttress, whilst in the field across, a series of boundary posts can be seen. Embossed M.R. they are manufactured from a length of old rail with the top section flattened, confirming that the Midland Railway once owned this water.

The canal turns sharp left to reach Gregory tunnel, the only underground section on this walk. It's 81 yards long with the towpath well paved, and has railing to prevent an accidental detour. In the field below the canal is half an old railway carriage, clerestory roofed. It's totally secluded but appears occupied if the garden chairs and washing on the line are any guide.

The quantity and variety of birdlife on this canal are most noteworthy. Little grebes, mallards and waterhens, and a whole range of hedgerow birds, all competing for the loudest noise, with at least two wrens drowning out the lot. Exquisite.

Thus far much of this walk is delicately tree lined as it clings to the hillside, but now the views open up dramatically as the woods are left behind. An aqueduct takes the water over the railway where the latter plunges into a tunnel. The canal, of course, went round the hill. On the skyline to the south-east at this point, Crich Stand is plainly visible. This memorial to the Sherwood Foresters stands

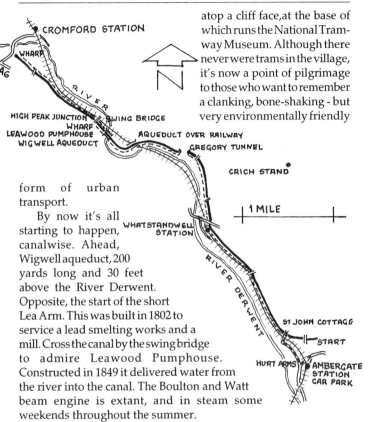

atop a cliff face, at the base of which runs the National Tramway Museum. Although there never were trams in the village, it's now a point of pilgrimage to those who want to remember a clanking, bone-shaking - but very environmentally friendly form of urban transport.

By now it's all starting to happen, canalwise. Ahead, Wigwell aqueduct, 200 yards long and 30 feet above the River Derwent. Opposite, the start of the short Lea Arm. This was built in 1802 to service a lead smelting works and a mill. Cross the canal by the swing bridge to admire Leawood Pumphouse. Constructed in 1849 it delivered water from the river into the canal. The Boulton and Watt beam engine is extant, and in steam some weekends throughout the summer.

An extensive wharf across the canal, with many carefully restored buildings, was the trans-shipment area for freight travelling the Cromford and High Peak Railway. There is one fearful tale told of an incident here in 1888. Two wagons broke free at the top of the incline, one fully loaded. They careered unrestrained down the hill. Eye witness accounts record that they were moving "a bit fast" by the time they reached the bottom. Crashing straight through the sidings, they are reputed to have launched themselves into the air, soaring over the canal, the farm track just to the right, and the main railway line before crashing back to earth. The mind boggles...

53

Another mile sees the end of the canal. Since the County Council took over the line this area has been conserved and is a popular spot with visitors. Several of the old buildings remain, some dating back to 1794. Toilets can be found in the right-hand corner. Leave the site, turn right and follow the road for $^1/_4$ mile to Cromford station.

Don't leave this area without taking the opportunity to explore some fascinating and rugged countryside all around, together with lots of attractions. This is a major tourist area. Matlock and Matlock Bath are both well worth a visit, whilst opposite the canal terminus is Arkwright's Mill. This belonged to Sir Richard Arkwright (1732-92) who, in 1771, first used water power here to drive a cotton mill. His home, Willersley Castle - known locally as Arkwright Hall - is close by. The National Tramway Museum at Crich, another working steam engine at Middleton Top, cable cars, castles and unsurpassed views all compete for your attention after the walk.

WALK 10 - NOTTINGHAM TO COTGRAVE - RIVER TRENT AND GRANTHAM CANAL

With such a choice of distances, this is a walk that ANYONE can enjoy. Because of the permutations, this walk will use public transport for the return leg rather than the more usual outer.

Coal was the motive behind the construction of the Grantham Canal. Linking the eponymous town with the River Trent and the Nottinghamshire coalfields would open up huge areas of Lincolnshire to cheap fuel. An Act was obtained in 1793, and the 33 mile cut with its 18 locks was ready for traffic throughout by 1797. Success inevitably followed, creating, as the promoters planned, a distribution net based on the basin in Grantham.

Just as inevitably, the coming of the railways saw traffic leave the water. Following a depressingly similar course of action the company sold out to the competition in 1854, creating a company that must have held some sort of record for the length of its name: the Ambergate, Nottingham, Boston and Eastern Junction Railway and Canal Company. Soon after, the Great Northern Railway took over operation as long distance trade continued to ebb from the water. Short distance traffic was still in evidence.

At the turn of the century some 20,000 tons of goods were still

Still lots of restoration work lies ahead on the Grantham Canal

being carried. One less pleasant aspect of trade was that night soil was moved from Nottingham to be spread on the surrounding fields. By the early 1930s the London and North Eastern Railway were in charge and trade had all but disappeared. They obtained an Act of Abandonment in 1936 but were forced to include provision for land drainage - the reason there is a canal here today.

The Grantham Canal Restoration Society Ltd. are hard at work pressing for full restoration, and are making good progress at the eastern end. Major problems do exist. Near Grantham the A1 trunk road provides a barrier. The canal from there to the town is in private hands, and unlikely to be restored. In Nottingham, as will become clear during the walk, major road works have created huge obstacles. But as other projects around the country have proved, nothing is insuperable today. One option currently being favoured is to reroute the line, using a new cut along the Polser Brook, rejoining the River Trent at Holme Pierrepont, there to construct a marina.

BEFORE YOU START

WALK DISTANCE: 1¹/₂, 2¹/₂, 4¹/₂, 5 or 6 miles

MAP: OS Landranger Series Map 129

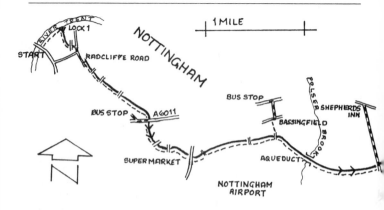

START:	Trent Bridge, Nottingham
PUBLIC TRANSPORT:	Intercity and National Coaches both serve Nottingham. The start is less than a mile away from the respective stations
STARTING GRID REF:	SK 582382
CAR PARKING:	Not good. Side streets nearby, but these are full when Nottingham Forest soccer or Trent Bridge cricket grounds are in use. If these sports grounds are going to cause a problem and you are sure of your choice of distance, it may be a good move to drive there and catch the bus into Trent Bridge. Each of the option points has easy parking close by
TRANSPORT:	Barton bus service 21 runs from Cotgrave to Nottingham and picks up at every option except the 2½ mile one. Alight at the end of Bridgford Road, just opposite the cricket ground, and only a few yards from Trent Bridge. For the 2½ mile one, Barton service 22 runs hourly, or Nottingham City Transport run four buses an hour past the entrance to Safeways. Full details of both services on 0115 924 0000
REFRESHMENT:	Everything at the start, cafeteria at 2½ miles (see text), pubs and shops at finish
NEAREST TIC:	1-4 Smithy Row, Nottingham NG1 2BY - 0115 947 0661

Trent Bridge to Safeway Supermarket - 2½ miles

On the south bank of the River Trent head downstream with the river on your left, along the appropriately named Trentside. This leads right under the new stand at Nottingham Forest's soccer ground and, after only a few more yards, to the start of the Grantham Canal. Here can be found the first lock. It has gates and paddle gear in full working order but it is stanked off from the river, with the chamber securely fenced, and has not been used since a rally in 1973. Turn right and follow the towpath.

SITE OF
COTGRAVE
COLLIERY

US
TOP

COTGRAVE

After 100 yards the canal is infilled. Turn right, along Ladybay bridge, across the traffic lights into Radcliffe Road and cross to the left-hand side. After 100 yards a gate gives access to the canal and towpath. This continues for some 400 yards before reaching the site of Rutland Road swing bridge. To get round this obstruction involves returning to the pavement. Another gate beyond allows the walk back to the canalside just beyond.

This section is clearly urban, with a very busy road alongside, but across the canal the housing is redolent of suburbia in the late 1930s, with long mature gardens reaching down to the water's edge. At the end of this section the canal swings to the right, giving the first opt-out.

(Turn right, cross the dual carriageway and take the first on the left - Davies Road. A bus stop is located a few yards down there on the left).

Cross the road, one half of a dual carriageway, and take the path opposite which leads under the far road. This is a widened old Grantham Canal bridge, the only extant one on this walk. A winding hole beyond, and the canal enters a more open area. The towpath here is awkward in that for some 300 yards it undulates, almost as though you were walking across a ridge and furrow field. Soon the next lock appears. Cascaded, the chamber itself is in good condition with only the copings missing, but there are no gates or paddle gear.

Fine new housing is now located on the left with a couple of canal crossings. These too were once swing bridges but are now fixed. Another lock and, as the canal swings to the right, the second opt-out point, the Safeway supermarket on the canalside. The cafeteria here is a useful mid-walk refreshment point.

(A bus from this supermarket will return you to the city.)

Safeway Supermarket to Cotgrave Bridge - 2½ miles

Shortly the canal reaches a busy dual carriageway where it is culverted. Cross the roads - taking care - and regain the towpath at the far side. This road makes the boundary between suburban Nottingham and open countryside. Fields now rule and Nottinghamshire at its gently undulating best unfolds before your eyes. Yet another flattened bridge at Tollerton follows and beyond, the canal straightens for a short while. At the end, just as the line is about to swing sharp right, a bridge crosses the water, offering the 4 mile opt-out point.

(Cross the bridge, walk into the hamlet of Bassingfield and turn right at the road. Immediately there is a left turn which leads to the main road and the bus stop, some 500 yards from the canal.)

Around the corner a small aqueduct takes the canal over the Polser Brook, and the possible new route to the Trent. The canal sweeps to the left before reaching another lockchamber. This one even carries its number - 5. Above, reed-mace grow in the centre of the water, the first time that the actual channel has not appeared navigable. At the flattened Cotgrave Bridge is the 5 mile opt-out.

(Turn left and walk down the road for about ½ mile to the Shepherds Inn, a Brewers Fayre establishment. The bus stops here, although you may well find that it is possible to flag one down should it appear before you reach the stop proper: very accommodating drivers in these parts!)

Cotgrave Bridge to Cotgrave Village - 1 mile

Across the road the towpath enters what appears to be a more hilly area, though these "hills" are man-made. On the left, until as recently as 1994, Cotgrave Colliery used to be located. It was one of the many closed, ostensibly because it was unprofitable. Once it had ceased production the buildings and winding gear were razed with almost indecent haste, and the spoil heaps landscaped. This has happened at several other canalside pits, notably the one at Rugeley on the Trent and Mersey.

More locks, and at the next bridge site - Hollygate Lane - turn right and walk into the village of Cotgrave. The main bus stop is actually in the village, outside The Manvers Arms.

Chapter 3:
Staffordshire

WALK 11 - STOKE-ON-TRENT TO KIDSGROVE - TRENT AND MERSEY CANAL

It would not be difficult to find a prettier walk than this, but a wealth of industrial interest with some greenery and fascinating canal infrastructure to finish make it well worth attempting. The towpath is good all the way.

There were once great coal deposits around this corner of Staffordshire. In addition, deposits of iron ore and limestone, marl and flint were worked. The basics for steel and pottery making together with fuel explains why those industries were established in this area. It also provides several graphic illustrations of the damage that mining subsidence has caused over the years. All along the walk there is evidence aplenty of this condition. A look at the history of the Trent and Mersey Canal will be found in Walk 13.

BEFORE YOU START

WALK DISTANCE:	6 miles
MAP:	OS Landranger Series No 118
START:	Kidsgrove railway station, off the A50 Stoke to Warrington road
PUBLIC TRANSPORT:	Intercity and National Coaches to Stoke-on-Trent, Regional Railway service to Kidsgrove
STARTING GRID REF:	SJ 837533
CAR PARKING:	(Pay) at the station, side roads close by
TRANSPORT:	Two trains an hour from Kidsgrove to Stoke, except on Sundays when they start running in the early afternoon. Local bus service No 24 - Meir leaves from Kidsgrove town hall, 300 yards away - frequent service. Details from 01782 747000
REFRESHMENT:	Everything in Stoke, pubs en route, pubs and shops in Kidsgrove

NEAREST TIC: Potteries Shopping Centre, Quadrant Road,
                      Hanley, Stoke-on-Trent ST1 1RZ - 01782
                      284600

THE WALK

At Stoke railway station leave the building and turn left. At the end
turn left, under the railway and on the right is access to Stoke lock.

Stoke Bottom Lock to Longport Wharf - 3 miles

This concrete cavern was constructed in the 1970s when 220 yards
of canal were diverted to accommodate a new road. Head up the
towpath under a low iron railway bridge and Cockshute lock. This
was once an interchange point, where wagonloads of pottery
materials were shunted alongside and trans-shipped by
wheelbarrow into waiting narrowboats. Also on this pound are a
couple of bottle kilns, the old way of baking pottery. Two more locks
- Twyfords and Johnsons - and a small arm on the right is home to
the Etruscan Bone and Flint Mill, suppliers of basic ingredients to
the pottery industry. Guided tours are available here.

The deep chambered top lock just beyond is Etruria where an
old dry dock stands alongside the British Waterways yard. Until
relatively recent times there was a roof over the top of this chamber,
but subsidence and the need to build up the bank created restricted
headroom, making demolition obligatory.

The Caldon Canal branches right, but the route on this occasion
is north; Walk 12 will explore this length of canal. Beyond the next
bridge on the left is the local newspaper office. This was once the site
of Josiah Wedgwood's pottery, in use until the last war. His house
stands atop the hill to the right. The heavy piling on the banks
indicates subsidence defence work, whilst looking down into the
newspaper works illustrates the effect graphically. The land here
was once level with the canal.

The towpath changes sides here for a few hundred yards,
crosses a lift bridge over the marina entrance and past the China
Garden pub. A century or more ago the canal continued in a straight
line, but the arrival of a railway created the need for a reroute. This
area was landscaped for the 1986 National Garden Festival out of
the sprawling dereliction that was Shelton Bar Iron and Steel
Works.

The rump of this once great business is on the left. Canopies used to overhang the canal, giving shelter to boats that once loaded here, but these disappeared in 1995. The long grey building that soon comes into view is the steel rolling mill with the crash of this process echoing around an otherwise quiet and remote section of canal.

Around a sharp left-hand bend, close to some white propane tanks, are the buttresses of an old railway bridge. In the days when Shelton Bar made steel, hoppers of molten slag trundled over this bridge to be dumped over the tip edge in a cascade of sparks and flame; a most impressive sight.

Here also was the Burslem Branch of the canal. This $1/2$ mile arm was only lost in 1961. Then a dramatic breach, again caused by mining subsidence, sealed its fate. At the time there was a narrowboat working on the banking, and this disappeared into the hole. Rather than attempt an awkward recovery, it was buried when the line was infilled. One day this will present an interesting find for future archaeologists on a dig.

The old building beyond bridge 124 was the Midwinter china works, one of many names now no more, redolent of a gentler age. Then a large canopy is seen. The tower beyond, with remains of a hoist, carries the legend THE ANDERTON CO. 1890, the base of one of the north's noted canal carriers. The next works identifies itself in large letters: Middleport Pottery. Built almost 150 years ago, boats unloaded clay at the Slip House to the south end. The manufacturing was carried out in buildings surrounding the central bottle kiln, a listed Ancient Monument, with the finished ware packed in the northernmost warehouse and loaded onto boats; an early case of time and motion study in operation.

Steelite Pottery comes next, makers of hotel ware. The next time you eat out turn the cup/saucer/plate upside down (preferably after emptying); you will probably see the company logo - a portcullis. Then Longport Wharf, now the home of Stoke-on-Trent Boatbuilders.

Longport Wharf to Harecastle Tunnel - $1^{1}/_{2}$ miles

The Duke of Bridgewater pub is by the bridge, and a chip shop close by. The last pottery to be seen on this walk has serried ranks of teapots visible through the windows, and their small bottle kiln still smokes occasionally, but only as the factory's rubbish is burned.

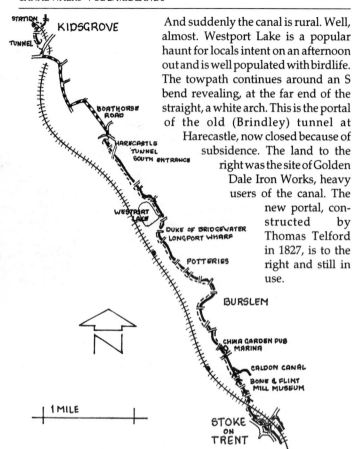

And suddenly the canal is rural. Well, almost. Westport Lake is a popular haunt for locals intent on an afternoon out and is well populated with birdlife. The towpath continues around an S bend revealing, at the far end of the straight, a white arch. This is the portal of the old (Brindley) tunnel at Harecastle, now closed because of subsidence. The land to the right was the site of Golden Dale Iron Works, heavy users of the canal. The new portal, constructed by Thomas Telford in 1827, is to the right and still in use.

Harecastle Tunnel to Kidsgrove - 1¹/₂ miles

As the towpath through the tunnel has been removed, the only way to continue is to follow (roughly) the track that the boat's horses once used. Just before the tunnel the towpath crosses to the right-hand side. Leave the canal here and walk up to the road. Turn left and at the junction a few yards ahead keep to the right up Hollywall Road. A few yards along is an unmarked road on the left called

Built for the National Gardens Festival in 1986, the China Garden is now a popular Potteries hostelry

Boathorse Road.

Follow this up and around to the left, through the gypsy encampment, and along an unmade road to the top. At A.J. Green's Meat Wholesalers turn right, follow the (now paved) road past The Rifleman pub, keeping to the left at each fork until arriving at a main road. Turn right and a few yards along a signpost on the left guides you to the northern portal of the tunnel.

If you can time your departure from the southern end to coincide with a boat entering the tunnel, you may well find that a brisk stroll over the top will get you to the other end in time to welcome the boat. A right turn will give the opportunity to examine the two northern portals. After, turn left, and beyond the railway bridge is a flight of steps leading to Kidsgrove station.

WALK 12 - ETRURIA TO STOCKTON BROOK
- TRENT AND MERSEY & CALDON CANALS

The most recent home of working narrowboats, staircase locks and an elegant city park alongside stark industry makes a quite irresistible walk. Because there is a choice of distance on this walk, the usual practice of utilising public transport on the outward leg is reversed.

The Caldon Canal was opened to Froghall in 1779, built by the Trent and Mersey company to carry limestone and flint from quarries in the hills to the hungry industry around Stoke-on-Trent. It was extended to Uttoxeter in 1811. Then in 1846 the Trent and Mersey was bought by the North Staffordshire Railway Company. They wanted to reach Uttoxeter, and the only route available beyond Frogall was along the route taken by the canal. That meant that the water had to go. It duly closed in 1847, replaced by the "iron horse". That left the original $17^{1}/_{2}$ mile length together with a 3 mile arm to Leek.

The North Staffordshire Railway and their successors maintained the canal quite well, and it continued to be used until after the last war. It was never officially abandoned, but became almost impassable by the 1960s. Being classified as a "Remainder" waterway by the 1968 Transport Act meant that British Waterways could only spend money on it for safety reasons. A canal society joined forces with two local authorities and British Waterways to effect restoration. With these combined forces it was very quickly finished, and reopened in 1974. Reclassification to "Cruising" standard was achieved in 1983.

Since then there have been several problems with the canal's bank, but it remains a stunningly beautiful canal at its furthest reaches,* and still underused by boater and walker alike. Indeed, the contrast between heavy industry at the start and sylvan beauty only a dozen miles away is a contrast unequalled anywhere else on the canal system.

---

* Two walks at the far end of the canal are described in this author's book *Canal Walks - North.*

Leawood pump house, Cromford Canal (Walk 9)
Harecastle Tunnel entrance, Trent & Mersey Canal (Walk 11)

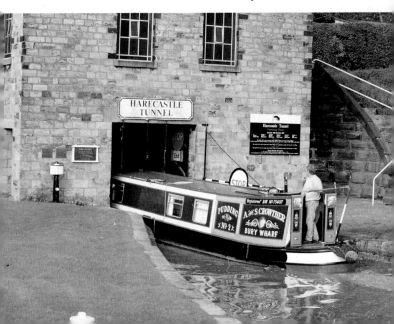

Coventry Canal near Whittington (Walk 14)
Wolverhampton bottom lock (Walk 16)

BEFORE YOU START

WALK DISTANCE: Etruria to Bridge 18, Milton - 4¹/2 miles Etruria to Stockton Brook - 6 miles

MAP: OS Landranger Series No 118

START: The China Garden pub, by Etruria Marina, to the north of the A53 Leek to Newcastle road

PUBLIC TRANSPORT: Etruria station on the Stoke to Manchester or Crewe lines is close by

STARTING GRID REF: SJ 869474

CAR PARKING: Plenty around the pub

TRANSPORT: Potteries Motor Transport service 218 Leek to Hanley covers both return points. Alight at Cobridge traffic lights and walk down the hill to Festival Park, about 600 yards

REFRESHMENT: At the start. Several pubs along the way

NEAREST TIC: Potteries Shopping Centre, Quadrant Road, Hanley, Staffordshire ST1 1RZ - 01782 284600

Etruria to Ivy House Lift Bridge - 2 miles

At the China Garden pub turn left. This was built in 1986 along with the marina as part of the National Garden Festival held that year. This whole area was derelict prior to the event, part of a steelworks. Now transmogrified to Festival Retail Park, it contains - boaters please note - a huge supermarket, multiplex cinema, and all the major retailers one would expect on this sort of development. The marina is a particularly attractive mix of private boats, hire fleet and restaurant boat in an entirely urban setting. This first section to Etruria Junction is walked the opposite way during Walk 11.

Just beyond the marina the busy dual carriageway forms a roving bridge. Arriving on the right-hand side, note the newspaper publishers, the site of Josiah Wedgwood's original works. Also look down on the small brick building. This domed-roof building was constructed in 1769, in the same style as the old bottle kilns that once belched smoke and fumes into the atmosphere here. Round, brick, and with a thick metal strap around its waist, it had a variety of uses over the years. The newspaper company restored it in 1985 to house a display of printing techniques used in both the newspaper and pottery trades. Once canalside, the whole area has suffered mining

65

subsidence.

Gone are the days when this area was a seething melee of boats delivering coal and clay to the pottery, and taking the finished product away to Liverpool docks for export. With the local steelworks, who were also extensive users of the canal, it really must have been something to behold.

Passing under the main road, Etruria Junction is soon reached with the Caldon Canal leaving to the left. Cross the footbridge just beyond the top lock to gain the new towpath. Two hundred yards into the walk, the canal makes a sharp right turn towards Bedford Street staircase lock. Until the winter of 1993/4 this was quite a narrow channel, but work was undertaken to widen it and re-enforce the bank. Above the two-chamber lock the housing is old and depressing, as are the factories; a really run-down area. Planet lock is next. With a 3ft 10in rise, this is a real oddity, not being built until 1916. Mining

66

The bottom gates of Bedford Street staircase locks, Caldon Canal

subsidence created the need for it.

There then follows a real oasis of green. Hanley Park is a well used recreation area very popular with locals. An overbridge signifies the return of the pottery industry. Until very recently narrowboats were in use here carrying commercially, but of the very interesting variety. Driven from either end they were used to take pottery a few hundred yards between two works of Johnson's Pottery. The operation ceased with the closure of the works in 1995, whilst a longer run to the Milton warehouse finished with rationalisation in the 1980s. Thus ended the last vestige of regular commercially used narrowboats, and with it, over two centuries of tradition.

Ivy House Lift Bridge to Milton - 2¹/₂ miles

Ivy House lift bridge signifies the end of the factories, This once had a fearsome reputation among boat crews, but sweat and effort have now been replaced by electric operation. Simply insert a key and press the button.

Before long a couple of sharp turns and the housing comes to an end. The canal is running along the side of the Trent valley and, whilst signs of civilisation are never far away, it can appear pleasantly rural - the more so for being so close to such a large city.

By bridge 16 the flattened factory on the left was where the working boats used to deliver. If pottery manufacture has undergone many upheavals in recent years, so too has the coal industry. Every colliery in this area is now closed, including Norton. The existence of this mine was the main reason for a 1,000 yard arm that ran off to the left alongside the Foxley pub. There was also an ironworks, but that too disappeared, and the infilled arm is now virtually impossible to trace. The pub is inaccessible from the towpath, but if refreshment is needed there are several pubs within a few yards of bridge 18 just around the corner.

At the next bridge (19) it is possible to conclude the walk, but if you have another $1^1/2$ miles left in you, there is increasingly attractive scenery to come.

Milton to Stockton Brook - $1^1/2$ miles

Four locks, two lift bridges and the canal's feeder from Knypersley reservoir to the north are offered in this short distance.

The housing at Milton is soon left behind as Engine lock is reached. This is very deep - over 12ft - and was so called because of a steam driven beam engine located close by which pumped water from a local mine. Beyond is a lift bridge, this time operated by hand.

As the canal turns slightly to the right, an arm disappears to the north. This is a feeder from Knypersley reservoir, 3 miles away. At this point look down in the valley below for a tiny stream. This is the infant River Trent that will eventually develop into England's second longest as it meanders its way for 170 miles through the heart of England before reaching the Humber and the North Sea.

Through increasingly pretty countryside, the canal heads east towards the next lock, Waterworks. Fens lock follows, which precedes a very low railway bridge. One more lock and the main road is reached. Here leave the towpath to catch the return bus.

WALK 13 - COLWICH TO STAFFORD - TRENT AND MERSEY & STAFFORDSHIRE AND WORCESTERSHIRE CANALS

This pleasant, almost entirely rural walk in the vale of the River Trent has most of the constituents of a good canal walk. There is a wide selection of canal infrastructure, good views and plenty of boating activity in season.

Two of the earlier English canals, both the Trent and Mersey and the Staffordshire and Worcestershire, were engineered by James Brindley. They were conceived as part of his scheme to create a "Grand Cross" over the country, linking the rivers Severn, Mersey, Thames and Trent. The 46 mile Staffordshire and Worcestershire was first on the scene, completed in 1772, the year of Brindley's death. It stretches from Great Haywood to the River Severn at Stourport, a town largely created by the canal. Here, traffic was trans-shipped into barges for forwarding to Bristol and beyond. It was ever a busy line, retaining a good level of trade through to the 1950s. Then coal from Cannock Chase to Stourport power station ceased, and the canal lay almost fallow until the leisure revival. It is a scenically pretty canal, as both this and Walk 28 will reveal.

The Trent and Mersey - or the Grand Trunk Canal as its progenitors were disposed to call it - was finally opened in 1777. The southern stretch, between Stoke-on-Trent and Shardlow on the River Trent, was open and trading by 1770, but the northern (Mersey) link was delayed by the need to construct a huge tunnel at Harecastle, north of Stoke - see Walk 11 - and a tricky section along the valley of the River Dane, near Middlewich. The instigator of this canal was Josiah Wedgwood, the potter. His factory at Stoke was suffering acutely from poor communications. Packhorse and carts were the only means of bringing clay from Liverpool and returning the finished ware for export. Needless to say, this rather rough and unreliable system resulted in huge losses through breakage. With the completion of the canal, transit times were reduced by 75 per cent and damage eliminated. It is no exaggeration to say that ease of transport occasioned by the canal age became the final piece that completed the jigsaw that was the Industrial Revolution.

And not only pottery gained. Coal, iron ore and salt were

frequent cargo along this canal, and the last trade lingered on into the 1960s, actually overlapping the arrival of pleasure cruising.

REMAINS
OF STAFFORD
BRANCH

TRUMPET

BEFORE YOU START

WALK DISTANCE:	7 miles
MAP:	OS Landranger Sheets 128 & 127
START:	The Trumpet pub, 1¼ miles from Stafford on the A513 to Rugeley
PUBLIC TRANSPORT:	Stafford is served by intercity rail and National Coaches
STARTING GRID REF:	SJ 939223
CAR PARKING:	The Trumpet (with permission) or side roads close by
TRANSPORT:	The 825 Midland Red service from Stafford to Lichfield and Tamworth stops outside the Trumpet. Enquiries on 01785 223344. Alight at Colwich by the church
REFRESHMENT:	Pub at the start and finish. Shops and pubs in Great Haywood
NEAREST TIC:	The Ancient High House, Greengate Street, Stafford ST16 2JA - 01785 40204

THE WALK

Colwich is just off the A51 Rugeley to Stone road. Across from the church where the bus stops are two paths to the right of the buildings. Take the right-hand one which soon reaches Colwich lock, Trent and Mersey Canal.

Colwich to Great Haywood Junction - 2 miles

Turn right and pass under the vast railway bridge where the lines to Scotland and Stoke-on-Trent diverge. It was here, in 1986, that an horrific train crash occurred when a northbound express turned right into the path of a London-bound train and the train crews were fatally injured.

Beyond and to the left the hills of Cannock Chase can be seen. There are over 20 square miles of heathland, designated an Area of

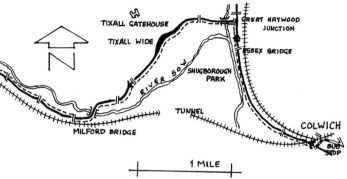

Outstanding Natural Beauty, with herds of fallow deer roaming wild. Ahead, a pretty (unnumbered) iron bridge spans the canal. This used to be the drive to Shugborough Hall which can be seen through the trees on the left. The River Trent is at the other side of the towpath here. Rhododendron bushes line the far bank, offering a spectacular floral display in the right season.

A little further along a delightful stone bridge can be seen crossing the river. But it is not all it seems from this angle. Closer examination reveals it to be a packhorse bridge, the largest in the country, and only about 4ft wide. The seventeenth century Essex Bridge was originally a 40 arch structure; now only 14 are left. It gives access to Shugborough Hall, a National Trust property of truly magnificent proportions, and very well worth a visit. It is the ancestral home of the Earls of Lichfield - photographer Patrick is the latest - and a "must" for anyone with even the vaguest appreciation of beauty.

Opposite Haywood lock is a house that used to carry a large notice threatening all kinds of mayhem to any boater daring to step on its ground. Now it is the Lockhouse Restaurant, licensed, offering hot meals all day, and bed and breakfast; altogether more welcoming. The elegant and much photographed bridge spanning the northern end of the Staffordshire and Worcestershire Canal can be seen now. This busy junction always has a collection of boats moored whilst the hire company across the way is a scene of frenetic activity at weekends as new holidaymakers replace the leavers.

The elegant Essex Bridge provides an entrance to Shugborough Hall

Great Haywood Junction to Milford Aqueduct - 2 miles

The walk turns left, into the Staffordshire and Worcestershire Canal. Its tortuous wanderings, a Brindley hallmark, can be seen almost at once. First, the line crosses over the infant River Trent on an aqueduct, and then under a bridge. Notice the large cast iron plates that carry not only the bridge number but its name as well.

The far bank then starts to move away as the canal enters a reed lined expanse known as Tixall Wide. A popular location for fishermen, it still retains a remarkable. collection of birdlife. Moorhens, mallards, herons, great crested and little grebes and kingfishers all use the Wide as home. Beyond are the stables and gatehouse of Tixall Hall. The original Tudor hall was sited here in 1580, built by Sir Walter Aston. A replacement was built alongside in the eighteenth century by Thomas Clifford, a descendant of the Astons. Mary, Queen of Scots was imprisoned here for a fortnight in 1586, only a few weeks before she met her end at Fotheringay. Although both halls are now long gone the newer building was there when the canal arrived. In agreeing permission for the cut to cross their land, the owners demanded a scenic passage; thus the broad expanse of water. The Gatehouse is now owned by the Landmark Trust, and is available for summer renting. At the far end is Tixall lock. A cast iron boundary post can be seen across the lock bearing the legend 'S.W.C.'.

A very pretty residence is situated across the canal by bridge 105, with swimming pool, greenhouse, and (seemingly) acres of carefully tended lawn. Swinging sharp left, the line crosses the River Sow on another heavily built aqueduct before turning right, avoiding the railway.

Milford to Radford Bridge - 3 miles

Trains here can creep up on you. There is a tunnel close by, masking the noise until the last minute. Walk alongside the railway for over a mile now. Predominantly rural still, at the far end are some attractive chalet type dwellings cut into the embankment. Several owners here have their boats moored outside the back door. As the canal makes a left turn under the railway, notice the concrete slabs in the towpath. Just here, a branch canal to Stafford used to exist. Baswich lock once took the canal down into the river, which was then canalised into the town. It's been abandoned and unused for many a decade.

The houses of Baswich now line the far bank, with the towpath side still offering unimpeded views to Stafford. Then trees start to obscure the view along the attractive last mile or so to Radford Bridge, number 98. Leave the canal here by the Trumpet pub.

WALK 14 - ALREWAS TO WHITTINGTON - TRENT AND MERSEY AND COVENTRY CANALS

Fradley Junction, where the Coventry Canal meets the Trent and Mersey is one of the more famous points in canal lore. Now it is the base of a respected hire fleet, the Swan pub, and an area always busy with people and boats. To walk here is something of a challenge because bus services locally are somewhat sparse but the extra

*A Trent and
Mersey milestone*

effort involved in fiddling with the local bus timetable is well worth it. A look at the history of the Trent and Mersey can be found in Walk 13 (p69).

The northern section of the Coventry Canal is unusual in that it was actually built by the Trent and Mersey. The Coventry's financial problems had seen construction finish in 1790 at Fazeley, near Tamworth, 11 miles away. The Birmingham and Fazeley Company, already open to Fazeley, urgently needed the Coventry's completion so that through traffic would be possible, adding desperately needed trade to their line.

With the consent of the impoverished Coventry directors, they took over construction north from Fazeley, eventually meeting with the Trent and Mersey construction team. For similar reasons they had obtained permission to build south from Fradley. With the line complete and tolls forthcoming, the Coventry were eventually able to buy back the Trent and Mersey section, but never the Birmingham and Fazeley length.

This strange state of affairs is evidenced today by the bridge numbering. This starts in Coventry - on Walk 20 - and reaches number 77 by Fazeley. From there subsequent bridges are named Birmingham and Fazeley style, until the line reaches Whittington 5½ miles along. There bridge 78 can be found.

The canal was immediately prosperous and continued to be used heavily long after the "Canal Age" had passed. Built to serve collieries, many remained in production well into this century, with narrowboats continuing to carry coal away. After that stuttering start shareholders eventually reaped rich dividends with good returns every year. Even in the last year before nationalisation - 1947 - 6 per cent was paid.

BEFORE YOU START

WALK DISTANCE:	7 miles
MAP:	OS Landranger Series No 128
START:	Lichfield bus station
PUBLIC TRANSPORT:	Intercity trains and National Coaches both serve the city
STARTING GRID REF:	SK 119093
CAR PARKING:	Not good centrally, but long stay parks on the edge of the shopping area
TRANSPORT:	Bus to Alrewas, and return from Whittington. Service details on 01543 252109
REFRESHMENT:	Pubs at each end, at Fradley Junction and Huddlesford Junction. Everything in Lichfield
NEAREST TIC:	Donegal House, Bore Street, Lichfield, Staffordshire WS13 6NE - 01543 252109

THE WALK

Alight at the post office at the crossroads of Main Street and Fox Lane in Alrewas and walk along Main Street up to the canal bridge.

Alrewas to Fradley Junction - 2 miles

This is Kents Bridge, number 48. Cross and turn left, continuing in that direction. The village cricket ground is on the far bank, but very close to the water's edge; many a ball must lie on the canal's muddy bottom after a lusty blow from willow blade.

75

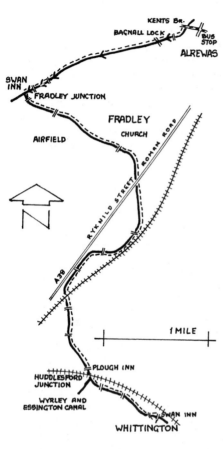

The first canal interest is just around the corner. Bagnall lock is preceded by a typically low and narrow bridge without towpath. The abutments carry scars from a thousand boats that missed the opening. An Ansells pub, the Navigation, is a few yards to the right, the first of several refreshment possibilities along this walk.

The main A513 passes overhead on a new bridge, but any noise pollution is soon behind as the walk heads into pretty remote countryside. The bulk of Cannock Chase rears up to the right in the distance. The '24 miles to Shardlow' post is passed at Common lock. These cast iron posts, unique in style, are to be found along the whole length of this canal. Over the years some have been lost or damaged. They were dug out for the duration of the Second World War as a security measure, but subsequently resited. Those lost were recast in 1977 by the Trent and Mersey Canal Society and are now in place.

The surrounding land starts to rise and the first of three locks that lift the canal to Fradley Junction follows. There are moored boats aplenty along this stretch, and the British Waterways yard. At Junction lock cross the water and turn left, past Wharf house, to the Coventry Canal.

Before crossing, you need to decide if you can resist the siren call of the Swan Inn, and the junction itself. Once a real canalside pub, the Swan is modernised and prettified, but still pleasant. Swan Line Cruises have a shop in the same block of buildings, stocking a range of the sort of goodies needed to sustain the inveterate canalside walker. They also offer maps, books, magazines, and canalware. Outside, a finger post installed jointly by the Coventry Canal and the Trent and Mersey Societies was unveiled by a former Inland Waterways Association chairman, the late Ken Goodwin, in 1986.

Fradley Junction to Huddlesford Junction - 4 miles

After the intimate little bridges typifying the Trent and Mersey Canal, the broader sweep of the Coventry version comes as quite a contrast. Fradley Junction is over almost as soon as it began and the walk heads south-east. To the right acres of flat land indicate the site of RAF Lichfield. This was a wartime bomber base. Lancasters and Wellingtons were flown from here by Commonwealth pilots. The RAF moved out in the 1960s, leaving a token presence until the 1980s when they gave it up completely. The hangars are now used for storage with agricultural fertilisers to the fore, and the road haulage industry have moved in to store surplus trailers. A percentage of the land has been returned to agricultural use, whilst some tarmac remains, used by a weird variety of flying craft; and some that look as though they never will, but do.

The towpath on this section is in fine condition, but little used with plenty of long grass. At the second bridge (90) a short detour to the right will bring you to Fradley church, a fine old building with an unusual corner in the graveyard. Neatly laid out are the last resting places of aircrew from all over the world, casualties from the airfield during the last war. Well tended, with clean cut headstones, it is a peaceful little section, made all the more poignant by the presence of one German name.

But peace soon becomes a casualty as the towpath brings the A38 dual carriageway ever nearer. This main traffic artery, carrying heavy lorries between the Midlands and South Wales and Yorkshire and the North East is a roaring torrent of noise. The old bridge is still in use, its concrete cousin alongside, resulting in variable headroom underneath: be warned.

The canal then takes a long right-handed sweep with a freight only railway line alongside, returning to run by the main road for a few hundred yards. At Lichfield Marina a small collection of boats marks the end of this straight length, and a left-hand bend takes the water away and back to something resembling peace and quiet.

And in almost a flash, the character of the line has changed. It's intimate again. The towpath has deteriorated markedly, and a short section offers something quite unusual: a line of fairly well established trees and shrubs between path and water, giving a feeling of being quite cut off from the canal.

The Plough at Huddlesford soon heaves into view. A toper's delight, this walk, with yet another famous waterside inn offering Ansells beer. Noise of a different kind intrudes here. The electric railway carrying the main line from London to Lancashire and Scotland passes overhead. Noisy, but somehow a more friendly sound than the road behind. Here also is the junction of the Wyrley and Essington Canal.

Huddlesford Junction to Whittington - 1 mile

The first few hundred yards of this canal are still in water, used as moorings by the Lichfield Cruising Club. Infilled then as far as Ogley Junction, 7 miles and 30 locks away, this used to provide a link with Wolverhampton, and would be a valuable addition to our existing cruising network were it ever to be reopened. Abandoned in 1954 there are people actively engaged in working out restoration proposals although there are massive problems to overcome. A proposed motorway is currently scheduled to pass over the canal's course which will do nothing to improve the prospects. The other end of this abandoned canal at Ogley is visited during Walk 15.

The last mile of this walk is through gently undulating countryside terminating at bridge 79 where another Swan Inn is located. Leave the towpath, cross the bridge and follow the road around to the left, and eventually back to the Bell Inn where the Lichfield bus stop will be found.

WALK 15 - CHASEWATER CIRCULAR - BIRMINGHAM CANAL NAVIGATIONS

The northern reaches of the Birmingham Canal Navigations are seldom reached by boats, yet contain some attractive water which is generally unpolluted and sustains a wide range of plant, fish and bird life.

A detailed look at the formation of the Birmingham Canal Navigations will be found in Walk 25. This walk takes in the Cannock Extension Canal, the Wyrley and Essington, and that canal's Anglesey Branch, all part of the Birmingham Canal Navigations.

The original canal in this area was the Wyrley and Essington. Opened in 1797 it provided a link between Wolverhampton and the Coventry Canal, and access to the south Staffordshire coalfield. The Anglesey Branch was originally conceived as a water feed, but was actually to carry the last commercial traffic around here which

Excessive weed growth on the Cannock Extension Canal shows the lack of boats using this short line

lasted until 1967.

The newest canal of the Birmingham Canal Navigations network was the Cannock Extension, opened in 1858 to draw trade from coalfields around Cannock Chase. It originally ran from the Wyrley and Essington to Hednesford, with a branch at Rumer Hill, to the Staffordshire and Worcestershire at Hatherton. At this junction were 13 locks, but the whole site has been mined for opencast coal, and no trace of this superb flight remains. The rest was abandoned in 1963, save this short section at the southern end.

BEFORE YOU START

WALK DISTANCE:	7¹/₂ miles
MAP:	OS Landranger Series No 139. The Birmingham A-Z Guide also covers all this walk
START:	Albutts Lane, Norton Canes. Travelling east along the A5 from the M6 at Junction 12, after 6 miles turn left at the traffic island (signposted Norton Canes) into Walsall Road. After a few yards a narrow turn to the right is Albutts Lane. 100 yards on the right is a car park
PUBLIC TRANSPORT:	Walsall is the closest
STARTING GRID REF:	SK 021072
CAR PARKING:	As above
TRANSPORT:	Not needed
REFRESHMENT:	Several pubs en route
NEAREST TIC:	Donegal House, Bore Street, Lichfield, Staffordshire WS13 6NE - 01543 252109

Albutts Lane to Pelsall Junction - 1¹/₂ miles

This car park is actually located on the bed of the canal. A path at the end of the car park leads back to the A5 along the canal's course. This is evidenced by brickwork to the left which used to form the towpath edge.

Cross directly over the A5 and pass through the gate. This gives access to the towpath, and canal which is in water after just a few yards. A collection of boats and waterside buildings indicate a boatyard: this was the old Malcolm Braine empire, a boatbuilder of

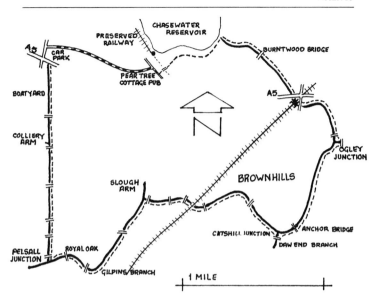

great repute. Curiously, virtually all the boats are traditionally styled, hardly a GRP or even a steel hulled cruiser style craft in sight. From here the canal is arrow straight right to Pelsall Junction.

The towpath is tree lined and, after a secondary road passes overhead and drifts away to the left, is quite peaceful. Two large arms to the right used to serve Brownhill Colliery, one brick building being the only link with the past. At the junction, the canal narrows through a toll area, and two Birmingham Canal Navigations houses still numbered 211 and 212 remain. The walk turns left here.

Pelsall Junction to Ogley Junction - 3½ miles

Cross Friars Bridge, very BCNish in cast iron with brick piers. Incidentally, this style of bridge, rather than the more normal arch, was built thus in mining areas so that they could be raised easily to counteract subsidence. The area to the south is grassed and well maintained; to the north, just scrubland. After 200 yards at Friars Bridge, the first refreshment stop is available. The Royal Oak serves Ansells beer and has a restaurant and steak bar attached. A keystone in the brick bridge is in badly weathered stone and engraved 1866.

Beyond the next bridge the canal turns sharp left, whilst on the towpath side was the privately owned Gilpins Branch. Originally about 1,000 yards long, it serviced collieries, and traces can still be seen by the diligent searcher. Countryside has returned to the left, but industry still makes its presence felt on the right side.

The tree lined depression after the next bridge is marked "cse of old rly" on the map, and after a short distance it climbed steeply to cross over the canal. The firm on the right is unusual; it manufactured blank graveyard headstones, polished and shaped, but sans inscriptions. To the right was a rather important private length of canal.

The Slough Arm provided transport to and from Coppice Colliery. It contained a shallow lock, was almost 1 mile long in total, becoming disused in the early years of this century. It's difficult to imagine now that this area was at the centre of the south Staffordshire coalfield, providing the great manufacturing city of Birmingham with the fuel it needed. Now there is scarcely a trace. On this section is a pleasant reminder of where we are. Concrete fencing posts alongside the towpath have the initials B.C.N. cast into them, as can be seen at Wolverhampton top lock on Walk 16.

The canal reaches the edge of Brownhills. And never does more than that; it skirts the town to the south and east, forming a natural barrier to development. The towpath side is unused; to the left, solid housing. At Catshill Junction cross the bridge over the Daw End Branch. A Birmingham Canal Navigations Society finger post points the direction of this walk. Both canals have narrows here, where toll booths were located. As boats passed, their load was gauged and tolls levied accordingly. At Anchor Bridge there is more chance of refreshment at the Anchor, which serves that doyen of Midlands ales, Banks's.

A few yards further was a junction with the Sandhills Branch heading left for 1 mile. There is no trace of this now, just open fields. The water is crystal clear and it is easy to spot shoals of fish. Its purity is confirmed by a choice of waterbirds living here; even the little grebe.

Head on into a shallow sandstone cutting and to Ogley Junction. The main line ran straight on here, down 30 locks to Huddlesford

Junction and Walk 14. Now the only option is to turn left over the bridge.

Ogley Junction to Albutts Lane - 2½ miles

An aqueduct takes the canal over a railway, one track in place, overgrown and rusted. Shortly after, the A5 is noisily overhead. At Burntwood Road bridge remains of coal chutes can be seen. Lorries would reverse to them and tip coal into the waiting boats.

The end of the Anglesey Branch is now in sight. Ahead is the bulk of Chasewater reservoir. Take the left-hand path up to water level and continue walking away from the water. Almost at the stadium, a finger post indicates a right-hand path. Take this back towards the water. There is a cafe here that is open at weekends and weekdays in the summer.

Chasewater is a spectacular place to linger awhile, particularly at weekends. There are huge numbers of yachts in action, wind surfers, water skiers; in fact, the world and its wife seem to gather here on a sunny Sunday afternoon. There is wildlife in abundance, although the appellation "wild" hardly seems appropriate for mallards, geese and waterhens that will feed from your hand. Indeed they could probably face a charge of demanding sandwiches with menaces.

Picking up the walk again, eventually, a high wooden fence is reached on the left. As this bears away left, follow it and at the end a bridge can be seen. This is over yet another old railway; except that this is a preserved line with the opportunity of another distraction. A few yards walk to the right will reveal railway carriages dating back to 1879, and an enchanting old steam engine of 1882 vintage.

Resuming the path, cross the old bridge, turn right into Hednesford Road, and after 100 yards bear left at the Pear Tree Cottage pub, another Ansells house. This is Albutts Lane, and the car park is 10 minutes' walk along.

WALK 16 - WOLVERHAMPTON TO BREWOOD - BIRMINGHAM CANAL NAVIGATIONS, STAFFORDSHIRE AND WORCESTERSHIRE & SHROPSHIRE UNION CANALS

Although this chapter is devoted to two walks using constituents of the Shrophire Union Canal, there are two other lines used to make up the first walk. Yes, three different navigations on one walk.

The first is the Birmingham Canal Navigations. A look at the history of this important canal will be found in Walk 25. The short section of Staffordshire and Worcestershire Canal - see Walk 13 - leads to the Shropshire Union Canals proper.

This was an amalgamation of several different canals in 1846. The one on this walk was the Birmingham and Liverpool Junction Canal which ran from Autherley Junction to Nantwich (Cheshire). Opened in 1835, engineered by Thomas Telford, it provided a much quicker and less heavily locked route between Birmingham and Liverpool. This pleased the Staffordshire and Worcestershire not one jot. Much of this trade previously travelled along their canal from Aldersley Junction to Great Haywood - See Walk 13 -where it used the Trent and Mersey Canal. In an attempt to recoup their losses, the company started to charge an exorbitant toll for use of their $^1/_2$ mile link between Aldersley and Autherley.

Much miffed, the Shropshire Union Canals promoted a Bill in parliament seeking permission to build a flyover from the lower reaches of the Birmingham Canal Navigations locks to their canal at Autherley. Seeing their toll income in danger of evaporating totally, the Staffordshire and Worcestershire reduced their charges to a more reasonable level, and the threat was dropped.

From Autherley, the canal carries its Telford parentage clearly by carving a generally straight line north. It plunges into deep cuttings and strides over valleys whilst the locks are arranged in flights; a much quicker canal for boatmen to use. It carried trade along its full length until the 1960s, and needed very little alteration to allow pleasure boats to use it.

BEFORE YOU START

WALK DISTANCE:	7¹/₂ miles
MAP:	OS Landranger Series No 139 & 127. Most of this walk is also covered by the Birmingham A-Z Guide
START:	Market Square, Brewood. This is just to the south of the A5, 4 miles south-east of Junction 12 of the M6
PUBLIC TRANSPORT:	Nearest is in Wolverhampton
STARTING GRID REF:	SO 917986
CAR PARKING:	On street in Brewood
TRANSPORT:	Green Bus service 2 to Wolverhampton leaves from Brewood post office - not Sundays. Service details on 0121 200 2700
REFRESHMENT:	Everything in Wolverhampton
NEAREST TIC:	18 Queens Square, Wolverhampton, West Midlands WV1 1TQ - 01902 312051

THE WALK

Alight in Queens Square and walk down Lichfield Street and across into Broad Street. Over the ring road and just before the railway bridge, the towpath is accessible on the left, through a pretty oasis of greenery and seats.

Wolverhampton to Lock to Aldersley Junction - 2 miles

Immediately ahead is the first of 21 locks that punctuate the canal from here to the junction. Known by the old working boatmen as the 'Ampton 21, they used to be alive with working boats. One of the last regular cargoes along this canal saw narrowboat tankers belonging to the carrying company of Thomas Clayton bringing oil from Ellesmere Port on the Mersey to Oldbury.

The houses on the right by the top lock carry quite high numbers. These were allocated by the Birmingham Canal Navigations to

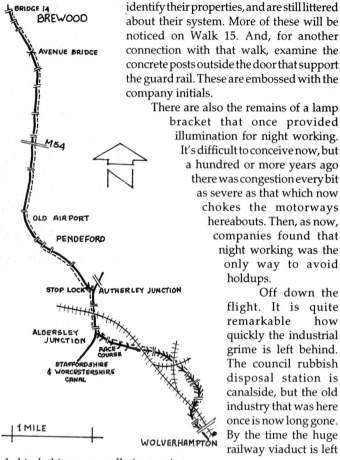

identify their properties, and are still littered about their system. More of these will be noticed on Walk 15. And, for another connection with that walk, examine the concrete posts outside the door that support the guard rail. These are embossed with the company initials.

There are also the remains of a lamp bracket that once provided illumination for night working. It's difficult to conceive now, but a hundred or more years ago there was congestion every bit as severe as that which now chokes the motorways hereabouts. Then, as now, companies found that night working was the only way to avoid holdups.

Off down the flight. It is quite remarkable how quickly the industrial grime is left behind. The council rubbish disposal station is canalside, but the old industry that was here once is now long gone. By the time the huge railway viaduct is left behind, things are really improving.

Wolverhampton racecourse is on the left. This was reconstructed in the early 1990s. Originally occupying a far greater area, the grandstand was rebuilt and the track realigned and covered with an all-weather surface. Now racing takes place here (almost) whatever the weather, often under floodlights.

A boat climbs towards Wolverhampton

Comparing the idyllic location of the bottom lock with its counterpart at the top is comparing chalk and cheese. This is set in total rurality, or so it seems. The Black Country is not too far away. At the junction, cross the Staffordshire and Worcestershire and turn right.

Aldersley Junction to Autherley Junction - ¹/₂ mile

Another huge railway viaduct, carrying the line to Shrewsbury, followed by a canal bridge. Here, on the left, a water inlet is reached. Dally not too long: this is the outflow from Wolverhampton sewage works. In the not too distant past, during times of drought when canal water was getting scarce, the old boatman's cry was reputed to be "Keep peeing Berningham [*sic*]!" In a rich Brummie accent, the local pronunciation of Birmingham had a certain ring to it.

Autherley Junction is now quite near. The line of boats and yard on the right was once home to a fleet of hire cruisers, but they disappeared towards the end of the 1980s. As the canal widens appreciably, a finger póst on the far bank points to the left, the direction of the walk.

Autherley Junction to M54 Motorway - 2½ miles

Just through the pretty white-painted brick bridge is a hive of activity. On the water is a shallow stop lock. This was built when the Shropshire Union Canals arrived here. It stopped the uncontrolled flow of water between the two canals, and gave the toll keeper, whose small cabin is alongside, the chance to capture every boat that passed. A hire fleet is also based here, and their boats are moored on both sides when not actually out working.

Another water inflow from the sewage works is passed as the canal leaves the junction. The third bridge is of the turnover variety, and the towpath moves to the right bank, where it will stay for the rest of this walk. Houses surround the canal. This is Pendeford, a huge estate that occupies what were green acres until the late 1970s. On the right was Wolverhampton airport. This was never a real commercial possibility with Birmingham so close, but it has a link with history. The factory building beyond the towpath is currently occupied by Dowty Aerospace, but during the war was owned by Boulton and Paul. They built the Defiant fighter there in the early years. In its own way this would have been a fine aircraft, but it coincided with the Spitfire and the Hurricane. Vulnerable to attack from below, and not as manoeuvrable as the latter two, it was fitted with an early form of radar and switched to night reconnaissance work.

There is a short section where the canal was excavated through a shallow cutting, and the red sandstone is clearly visible. But for the most part the countryside is open and fairly flat, and whilst the views are certainly not spectacular, they are bucolic Britain at its best. Acres of arable fields, attractive brick bridges and solitude, apart from a short section where the M54 buzzes its angry way across.

M54 Motorway to Brewood - 2½ miles

Entering a cutting, a bridge very different from its predecessors hoves into view. Built of stone with an elegant balustrade, the gracefully curved classical lines bespeak something rather special.

Avenue Bridge was built at the behest of the Giffard family. The canal was cut through their land, severing the road to Chillington Hall, the Giffard's ancestral home from the twelfth century. They wanted an attractive bridge, and they certainly got it.

A short distance to the left is Giffard's Cross, a road junction that actually has a wooden cross. This marks the spot where in 1513 Sir John Giffard killed a panther with his crossbow. The animal, a gift to Sir John, had escaped from its cage and was threatening to kill a woman and her child. The Hall, where Charles II rested after the Battle of Worcester in 1651, has been rebuilt over the years. The latest was started in 1724 and finished by 1785. It has an elegant Georgian front, and was designed by Sir John Sloane.

After the next bridge, the village of Brewood is visible on the right. Continue to bridge 14, in another wooded cutting, and walk up to the road. Turn right, pass the Bridge Inn and walk along this road to the centre of the village.

WALK 17 - WILLEY MOOR TO WHITCHURCH - LLANGOLLEN CANAL

The Llangollen Canal, part of the Shropshire Union network, is the most popular in the country for boaters. On foot it is difficult to find any return transport, normally reducing any visit to out-and-back strolls. However, the restoration of the short arm at Whitchurch does open up the opportunity to take a $5^{1}/_{4}$ mile walk along some of this beautiful line. The upper reaches of this canal are visited in this author's *Canal Walks - North*.

That we still have a canal here at all is fortunate. In 1944 the LMS Railway, owners of much of the canal system in Cheshire, Shropshire and the Midlands, applied for - and got - permission to close vast tracts of unused canals. Had it not been for the fact that the Llangollen was used to carry water from the River Dee in the Welsh hills to a reservoir at Hurleston, near Nantwich, a similar fate would have overtaken this canal.

This section was opened in 1805 as something of an afterthought: an expedient to solve what was becoming an intractable problem. The original plan was for canals to link the River Mersey at

The unusual frontage of the lock keeper's cottage at Grindley Brook allows a panoramic view of the flight

Netherpool (now Ellesmere Port) with the Severn at Shrewsbury. There was some formidable terrain to cross, and the work was carried out in disparate sections.

By 1795 the easy section between Netherpool and Chester was operational. A year later a section from Frankton to Llanymynech limestone quarries was finished, extended to Carreghofa where it would shortly link with the Montgomeryshire Canal's Eastern Branch at the pretty locks there. By 1801 the Frankton to Trevor section was complete. Work beyond Trevor, on the hilly section, had been carried out intermittently from 1796 but four years later, with just a short section to the north-west of Wrexham complete, the plans to reach Chester via Ruabon were abandoned. This saw the company in desperate straits: lots of canal already built, but going nowhere.

At that time a branch from Ellesmere to Whitchurch was under construction, and suggestions that a link from that to the Chester

Canal, near Nantwich, could be built quite cheaply were seized upon. This would give the much sought after access to the rest of the system. Reaching Shrewsbury still exercised the minds of the promoters, but the link was never completed.

With the start of leisure boating, the beauty of this canal placed it at the top of anyone's list of places to cruise. It has remained that way to this day.

BEFORE YOU START

WALK DISTANCE:	6 miles
MAP:	OS Landranger Series No 117
START:	Whitchurch (Shropshire)
PUBLIC TRANSPORT:	Regional Railways serve Whitchurch, as do National Coaches
STARTING GRID REF:	SJ 543415
CAR PARKING:	Adjacent to the bus station
TRANSPORT:	Four different operators run services C58, C59, C61, C61 C65 and 12 between Whitchurch and Chester. Buses average out at about one every hour. Full information on 01244 602666. There is no service on Sundays or public holidays.
REFRESHMENT:	Everything in Whitchurch. A pub serving excellent meals at the start of the canal section, another one a few yards off the water in Grindley Brook, and a canalside shop selling pretty well everything a few yards beyond
NEAREST TIC:	The Civic Centre, High Street, Whitchurch, Shropshire SY13 1AX - 01948 664577

THE WALK

The bus heads north towards Chester, crossing the canal at Grindley Brook. Ask the driver to put you off at the Blue Bell pub, about a mile further along. This stop will probably be on the main road at a crossroads as the bus carries on down the new road. A few services actually divert through the settlement that is Bell o' th' Hill, but the drivers seem thoroughly laid back about the whole thing, and will almost certainly stop at the junction for you.

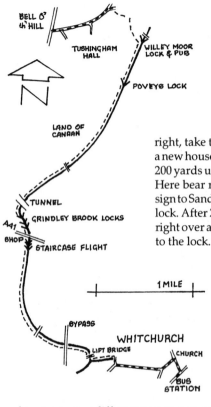

Bell o' th' Hill to Grindley Brook Bottom Lock - 3 miles

Cross the road and walk down the lane opposite heading south-east, turning first left after a few yards. At the bottom of this hill, where the road turns sharp right, take the lane straight ahead, past a new house on the left, and continue for 200 yards until you reach New Cottage. Here bear right following the footpath sign to Sandstone Trail and Willey Moor lock. After 20 yards another sign points right over a stile into a field which leads to the lock. Turn right at the towpath.

The Willey Moor pub here is right alongside the lock chamber, and is a fine place to refresh yourself after the strain of walking so far(!) But who needs an excuse? The beer is good and there is an extensive menu available should food be a priority. Beware though; winter opening hours are very different to summer ones.

Several years ago there was a spat here that made the national press, and left British Waterways with a modicum of egg on their corporate faces. Figures quoted in the story are all obtained second-hand and possibly exaggerated/underplayed to suit the teller's purpose. The story revolves around a metal bridge over the tail of the lock. It was installed in the 1970s by the pub's owners who had approached British Waterways and were given permission, agreeing to pay £50 per annum for the right. Prior to that, the only way across the canal was to use the lock gate; not the best plan after an evening spent imbibing their particular brand of "loudmouth soup". After 20 years the agreement came up for renewal. British Waterways decided that the fee would increase to £10,000!! As that was considerably over the net profit from the business, the invitation to renew was declined. Long and refractory negotiations did produce an agreement, although no-one is saying what!

The canal here is pretty, but a main road a few yards beyond the canal can be a little intrusive as heavy lorries thrash up and down. After another lock - Poveys - the canal strikes away from the road to Whitchurch, and into really peaceful surroundings normally associated with the Llangollen Canal.

A tunnel now appears. This was actually a massive railway embankment that used to carry the Whitchurch to Chester line. Like so many others it fell to the Beeching cuts of the 1960s. Here also is a county boundary. The walk starts in Cheshire, but above Poveys, the canal forms the divide between that county and Shropshire. The county line continues south-westerly as a sharp left curve beyond the tunnel brings the walk to the first of the Grindley Brook flight of locks.

Grindley Brook Bottom Lock to New Mills Lift Bridge - 1½ miles

This can be a place of much chaos in high season. There is very little room for boats to manoeuvre. The lock being emptied combines with the usual heavy flow of water from the by-wash to create much turbulence in this restricted space, to the regular consternation of boat crews.

After this there are another two chambers, each with equally fierce by-washes creating further problems for boats before a low road bridge with the staircase 3 lying just beyond. If there was chaos behind, there is certain to be even more here, albeit of a more organised type. The sheer numbers of boats wanting to pass this flight can sometimes mean a wait of well over an hour.

The staircase lock is different from a normal one in that, going up, the top gate of the chamber also acts as the bottom gate for the second lock. It is not possible to pass boats in the lock, so a system operates whereby the keeper will set the locks in one direction and work boats through non-stop that way for perhaps half an hour. Then he will turn the levels round so that the accumulated boats at the far end can pass through. Originally devised as the way to create a steep fall in a short distance whilst saving water, the idea is not the best in practice. Delays at this flight during the season are almost inevitable, as witnessed at Foxton during Walk 3.

The busy shop alongside the locks carries an extensive range of gifts and goodies with a chance to buy ice-cream, or any other canal walking necessities.

Beyond the staircase and boats waiting for locks, or using the water, sewage or rubbish facilities, the canal wanders off into a quiet section that is undisturbed for almost a mile until a new road, carrying the Whitchurch bypass, roars across a bridge overhead. The towpath, previously excellent, deteriorates a little along this section but is still comfortably passable.

New Mills Lift Bridge to Whitchurch - 1½ miles

At New Mills lift bridge turn left to walk alongside the restored Whitchurch Arm, until you reach the end. As constructed, the canal ran from Ellesmere to Grindley Brook. The town thought this was too far away, and campaigned for the canal to be brought closer. They succeeded in 1808, and a further extension was made in 1811. Abandoned in 1944, it was infilled with rubbish over the years.

Restoration plans were mooted over many years, and in 1982 Whitchurch Town Council took an interest. In 1993 Phase One of the plan was completed, reopening the canal just a short distance. The opening ceremony was performed by that great racehorse Red Rum, whose retirement home until his death in 1995 was only a few miles away at Cholmondley. As for the future, the bed of the old route has been built upon, and a new line is to be used. This ambitious scheme will include an inclined plane instead of locks to lower the boats towards the town.

At the end of the arm, leave the canal up a flight of steps, cross what will be a bridge again when the water is extended, and at the road ahead turn left. Follow this road until you reach a left turn along Yardington. At the end of here, in front of the Parish Church of St. Alkmund, turn right and walk down High Street through the centre of town. At the bottom turn left and cross the road. A few yards along on the right is an arcade of shops. Down here at the far end is the bus station, with the car park beyond.

WALK 18 - LAPWORTH CIRCULAR - GRAND UNION & STRATFORD CANALS

Into the depths of rural Warwickshire for this delightful walk. Although fairly short it still manages to pack in two separate canals, one of which boasts just about the newest length of water in the country, lots of infrastructure including some unusual canal houses and a few locks. In addition, it is well furnished with pub stops, so this stroll needs a good allowance of time. Notes on the history of the Stratford Canal will be found in Walk 23, those concerning the Grand Union Canal in Walk 2.

One slight identification problem in this area is the way in which villages run into each other. The start is midway between Lapworth and Kingswood. Although the canal junction is close to Kingswood and thus named, the road signs insist that it is Lapworth. A similar confusion is to be found at the end of the second leg. Is it Rowington or Turners Green?

There is an element of road walking in this walk, which enables it to be of a circular nature and does not rely on the somewhat sparse local transport.

BEFORE YOU START

WALK DISTANCE:	4¹/₂ miles
MAP:	OS Landranger Series No 139
START:	Canalside car park at Lapworth, Warwickshire, on the B4439 from Hockley Heath to Warwick. The parking area is carefully concealed in trees. Approaching from the Warwick direction, cross the canal bridge in Lapworth and turn immediately left along an unmarked road that services a few houses. There is a gap in the hedge to the left

Stratford Canal lock near Finwood. Note the unusual barrel shaped roof of the lock cottage

	which gives way to a clearing. On site are picnic tables and toilets
PUBLIC TRANSPORT:	Centro Trains serve Lapworth station. The nearest coach point is Warwick
STARTING GRID REF:	SP 186709
CAR PARKING:	As above
REFRESHMENT:	Pubs en route, as noted
NEAREST TIC:	Civic Square, Alcester Street, Redditch, Worcestershire B98 8AH - 01527 60806 or The Court House, Jury Street, Warwick, Warwickshire CV34 4EW - 01926 492212

Kingswood Junction to Rising Bridge - 1¼ miles

The car park gives onto the canal path, the northern section of the Stratford Canal. Turn left, and immediately the locks start. After passing lock 15 there is a road bridge ahead. Pass under it, turn left

The Stratford Canal (Walk 18)
Hatton Locks, Grand Union Canal (Walk 19)

Hawksbury Junction, Coventry Canal (Walk 20)
The walker's way over the Wootten Wawen aqueduct on the Stratfo
Canal (Walk 23)

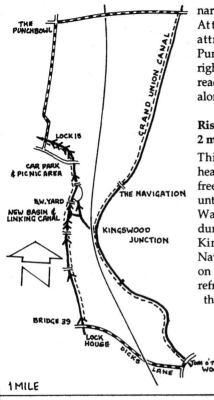

narrow, pretty country lane. At the end, on the left, is a very attractive pub called The Punchbowl. The walk turns right, crosses the railway and reaches the canal. Turn right along the towpath.

Rising Bridge to Rowington - 2 miles

This is the Grand Union heading south along a lock-free section that will continue until the great drop down to Warwick that is explored during Walk 19. Approaching Kingswood Junction, The Navigation Pub is reached, but on the non-towpath side. If refreshment is needed, leave the towpath at the bridge and cross over to it.

Looking right at the junction it is possible to see the new length of canal referred to earlier. It is also not many yards away from the start. In due course the walk will pass much closer to the length, and its significance will be mentioned then.

Into a most pretty length now. Trees, gently undulating hills and a canal that twists and turns, continue to hold the interest. Pass under bridge 63 and turn left to leave the canal. Across the way is another pub, oddly named Tom o' the Wood. According to the landlord this is named after a windmill which once ground flour in the area, but has now long gone.

97

Rowington to Kingswood Junction - 1¹/₄ miles

Turn left down the narrow lane and after 20 yards take the right-hand turn named Dicks Lane. Pass under the railway, and as the lane ends, turn right alongside the Stratford Canal at bridge 39, and lock 25. Having gained the towpath, pause for a moment and turn to look at the house you have just passed. The curious barrel-shaped roof on the original part of the building is unique to the Stratford Canal.

There are several examples along the southern section, including one close to Kingswood Junction. There has been a debate over the years as to why they were built thus, but no satisfactory explanation has been offered. The most likely one is that they were built by the canal's bricklayers who were used to creating arches when they built bridges, and adopted that same technique here.

The towpath continues along a very pretty section of canal with four more locks before the end of the southern section. Just below the last lock, the canal has been widened to accommodate a new(?) length of canal. Whether it qualifies for that label is open to debate. There was once a link here, but it has been filled in for many years. This cut now allows direct access to the Grand Union Canal without having to pass through the lock ahead, make an acute right turn and drop down another lock.

Beyond Kingswood Junction there is a wide lagoon to the right which acts as a reservoir for the southern section, and, a few yards further along, the turn back into the woods and the car park. For those who enjoy a barbecue, there are three thoughtfully provided.

WALK 19 - ROYAL LEAMINGTON SPA TO HATTON - GRAND UNION CANAL

Castles, spas and locks are all on offer during the course of this walk. Royal Leamington Spa and Warwick dominate the first half, but beyond, the scenery takes on an altogether more country aspect as you easily out-pace the boat crews sweating up the Hatton flight of twenty-one locks.

This canal was built by the Warwick and Birmingham Company and opened in 1800, linking Birmingham with the Oxford

This unusual letter box, in the style of a Doric arch, is in Warwick

Canal at Napton. The locks were narrow - 7ft - when built. After the Grand Union was formed in 1929, a modernisation programme saw the locks rebuilt as barge locks - 14ft.

The Hatton flight, known as "The Stairway to Heaven", was re-opened in 1934 by the then Duke of Kent. The aim was to bring a rationale to the line, and enable a last ditch improvement effort to be launched in an attempt to stem the flow of traffic away from water to both road and rail. The plan was to create a 70 ton barge canal, but the work was not complete when government cash ran out, and the narrowboat was never effectively replaced.

Further information on the Grand Union is contained in Walk 2.

BEFORE YOU START

WALK DISTANCE: 7 miles

MAP: OS Landranger Series No 151

START: Hatton rail station, which is to the south-west of Hatton village, on the A41 between Warwick and Solihull

PUBLIC TRANSPORT: As above

STARTING GRID REF: SP 224664

CAR PARKING: At the station

TRANSPORT: Train direct to Royal Leamington Spa. There is a good train service on weekdays, but nothing on Sunday

REFRESHMENT: Leamington, choice of pubs en route

NEAREST TIC: Jephson Lodge, Jephson Gardens, The Parade, Royal Leamington Spa, Warwickshire CV32 4AB - 01926 311470 or The Court House, Jury Street, Warwick, Warwickshire CV34 4EW - 01926 492212

THE WALK

Leave Leamington station on the south side, cross the road and head left towards the crossroads. Turn right here into Tachbrook Road, and the towpath entrance is just 70 yards along. If you like to combine your canalside walk with a general look around the area, you will need to go a long way to find a more interesting spot than Royal Leamington Spa. History abounds. A saline spring was noted here back in 1586, and Spa added to the name. The prefix Royal was awarded in 1838 after Queen Victoria had visited the town, and it has been a fashionable health resort ever since. The Regency Shopping Arcade offers traditional, speciality shops; more up to date is the Royal Priors Shopping Centre with a range of more modern stores. The Royal Pump Room, not currently open to visitors, is only one jewel amongst many.

Royal Leamington Spa to Budbrook Junction - 3½ miles

The start of the walk is through probably the less attractive part of the town. Older houses and, later, factories crowd the towpath for the first ½ mile before falling behind after the new road bridge is

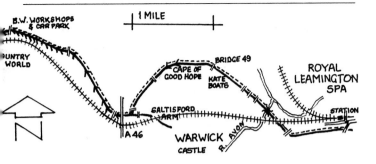

reached. There is also a busy road, but the fact that the canal drops into a cutting improves that problem.

Some new housing has been built on the left-hand side, a good, thoughtfully designed waterside development, the woodwork painted in a variety of garish colours. Mooring bollards and attractive paving all add to the impression, with an attempt to imitate warehouse construction providing the icing on the cake. A garden centre on the towpath side here is home to a wide range of gnomes, bird baths, and assorted concrete products with which to beautify your patio or lawn.

There is a short respite from buildings beyond bridge 44. The line passes over a railway track, and the River Leam closes in momentarily before sweeping away to its confluence with the Avon a hundred yards further along. That river then passes under the walk on a very well constructed aqueduct, and Warwick itself starts to dominate. On the towpath side is a building that has sustained many a canalside walker: the Fleur-de-Lys pie factory. The olfactory senses are teased unmercifully for a few yards before fresh air again rules. Small factories line the towpath whilst a boatbuilder constructing wide beamed craft occupies the far side, followed by Kate Boats, an esteemed hire fleet.

If Leamington was interesting, Warwick is dramatic. The canal passes to the north of the most interesting parts, but a brief detour from bridge 49 is recommended.

St. Johns House has displays based on the social history of the county. The Doll Museum is just that, and is capable of bringing a

101

glint to the eye of even the most macho of men, and Warwick Castle, a longish walk, is truly magnificent. Claimed (justifiably) to be the finest medieval castle in England, there is an almost endless list of attractions. The 60 acres of gardens and grounds were laid out by Lancelot Brown (aka Capability).

The real canal interest starts now beyond Warwick. The two Cape locks with the attendant Cape of Good Hope pub are first. Many a good yarn has been spun in this pub as boaters relaxed after the descent of Hatton, teasing those who were about to attempt the assault. A gentle curve with greenery to the right brings the Saltisford Arm into view on the left, now partially restored and occupied by the Saltisford Trading Company who operate moorings here.

Budbrook Junction to Hatton - 3$^{1/2}$ miles

Around the corner are Hatton locks: 21 broad beam chambers, each consuming 50,000 gallons of water every time they are used, occupy the next 2 miles, and will lift the canal 146ft towards the Birmingham plateau. The old (narrow) chambers are still extant by most of the locks, although now cascaded.

A garage halfway up the flight thoughtfully provides an entrance to the canal. With a well stocked shop, it is a boon to both boater and walker. Several houses here have splendid gardens, well maintained, and right down to the towpath.

Very little evidence can now be found of Asylum Wharf. There, on the towpath side, boats used to unload (mainly) coal for the hospital across the road, a trade that lasted until after the last war. British Waterways have their workshops at bridge 54, which takes the towpath to the left-hand bank. Pause awhile on the bridge and look back down the flight. It gives a superb view over Warwick, with the spire of St. Mary's church prominent.

Four more locks see the top of the flight reached. There is a handy canalside shop selling the usual small gifts, ice-cream and other basic refreshments. There is also a British Waterways display telling the story of the canal and Hatton locks. Sadly, the photo captions contain two real howlers!

A steam train is pictured on the railway nearby, and the locomotive is proudly proclaimed to be the ex LNER streamliner *Mallard*, holder of the world speed record for steam traction. The truth is somewhat more mundane. It actually depicts an LMS Railway freight engine which would probably have been shaken into its constituent parts had it travelled at much over half the speed record. Another picture shows Hatton locks being rebuilt: the view is actually Knowle, the next flight up the line!!

At bridge 55 a Nature Trail is signposted away from the canal. This leads to Hatton Country World, a 100 acre haven of rural attractions that includes rare farm animals, pets corner, and an enormous craft centre. Another 10 minutes' or so walking and bridge 56 sees the end of the walk. Leave the towpath, and across the road is the drive to Hatton station.

WALK 20 - COVENTRY TO HAWKESBURY - COVENTRY & OXFORD CANALS

The southern end of the Coventry Canal is one of those little used stretches of water that most people seem to avoid - either by accident or design - as travellers to and from the Oxford Canal tend to turn at Hawkesbury Junction. So, if not by water, why not by foot? Although largely urban, there are lengths of the walk that are green and peaceful, and it is never without interest.

This section was one of our earlier canals. The Coventry Canal Company opened their first stretch, between the city and Bedworth, in 1769. Water transport was already in use around the collieries in the area, and these were linked together by the newcomer. The subsequent history, shortage of money and the delay in completing their line is told in Walk 14.

Coal mines and links with the Trent and Mersey and Oxford canals kept the Coventry company thriving, and it was profitable right up to nationalisation.

BEFORE YOU START

WALK DISTANCE:	6½ miles
MAP:	OS Landranger Series No 140
START:	On the B4109 Coventry to Bulkington road at Hawkesbury

PUBLIC TRANSPORT:	Coventry is well served by coach and train from all around the country
STARTING GRID REF:	SP 363839
CAR PARKING:	Roadside near the start
TRANSPORT:	Bus to Coventry. Details on 01203 8323030
REFRESHMENT:	Several pubs en route
NEAREST TIC:	Bayley Lane, Coventry, West Midlands CV1 5RN - 01203 832303

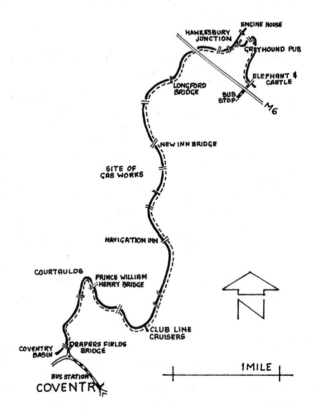

THE WALK

Directly underneath the M6 motorway bridge is the bus stop for Coventry. Alight in the city centre in Trinity Street, walk back to the first crossroads, and turn left into Hales Street. You may want to allow a little extra time around here because you will shortly pass the entrance to the Museum of British Road Transport.

This fascinating exhibition of old vehicles both famous and obscure is a "must" for anyone with the slightest interest in transport - even if it has nothing to do with canals. Beyond the museum turn right into Bishop Street and walk up the hill, cross the bridge over the ring road and bear to the right where the entrance to the canal basin can be found at the junction of Leicester Row and St. Nicholas Street. Coventry Basin has changed beyond recognition in recent years. Once a down-at-heel area, there has been an extensive development programme that has managed to complement the existing warehouses without overpowering them too much.

Aim for the left-hand side, through the gate where an old weighbridge is still in place: to weigh 10 tons. Clearly a remnant of horse and cart days; today's juggernaut carries that amount on one axle. The shape of the building is curious, being circular at the front, narrowing towards the back. There was another weighbridge on the other side, but there is now no sign of it. The new buildings ahead are being put to a variety of uses, but as yet there is no pub, although one is planned.

Enter the basin area and walk along the central isthmus to a new swing bridge. Cross this to the left and walk towards the Grade II listed bridge at the far end of the basin, past the new shops. There is a new sanitary station, another attempt to encourage boats to visit and add a purpose to the place. At the end of the buildings a road leads off to the left and slightly uphill. Follow this to the top and turn right over the aforementioned bridge, known as Drapers, and turn left to gain the towpath.

Coventry Basin to Old Church Road Bridge - 4 miles

This is a quite pleasant area of the city that has been landscaped. It is clean and tidy, with mooring rings for boats, and an old waterside crane. Before long, though, industrial Coventry asserts itself with factories lining both sides of the water. The towpath quality is

A few yards away from the redeveloped Coventry Basin is this listed bridge

excellent with a hard packed crushed limestone surface.

After bridge 2 there is a sharp right-hand bend with an enormous Courtaulds factory on both sides. Here too is the first milepost giving figures of 1 and 26: back to the Basin or Fazeley Junction. The overall impression along this stretch is one of surprising cleanliness and tidiness, two words that do not usually spring to mind when discussing an urban canal. British Waterways and the local Canal Society are working well here. Bridge 3, Prince William Henry, looks to have been in place for ever, but is uncommonly wide, carrying the main A444 into the city. Briers and brambles along the towpath beyond indicate rurality, not usual in the middle of a large place like Coventry.

But if the visual aspect is pleasing, noise pollution slowly becomes absolute. Round the corner, across the water is a scrapyard which processes old cars, compressing them into tiny bales. The walk moves along, away from it; houses close by have it all the time. This housing continues close to the water, but there are still enough trees to keep the whole thing quite pleasing.

By the 2 mile marker is a Birmingham Canal Navigations style bridge over an arm. Here Club Cruisers have taken up residence, the basin packed (in winter at least) with hire boats. The company also manufactures a range of boats for sale, and the whole compact yard has an air of business about it. Across the water are several other boats moored which have some connection with the business.

Bridge 5 brings a few hundred yards of utter seclusion with willow trees overhanging the water and knee high grass. Most agreeable. Soon, however, a housing estate intrudes, though with it comes a refreshment opportunity at the Navigation Inn. Notice the edge of the abutment here. An iron post protects the brickwork from rope damage, but has suffered severe scoring itself over the years.

There is another pub at the next bridge, Old Church Road. This one, the Royal, is an M & B house, a popular Midlands brew.

Old Church Road Bridge to Hawkesbury Junction - 2 miles

Beyond, on the right, the old industry has been swept away, and a modern retail park has arisen from the ashes. Across the water the remnants of Coventry gasworks remain. Gas holders are still in use, but the wide lay-by and unloading area for narrowboats are overgrown and neglected. In time gone by, this section of canal was knee deep in narrowboats bringing in coal from local collieries. But time moves on, and the old industries die. Now, there is hardly a colliery left in the area producing coal, and of course all the gas now comes from under the sea.

The Black Horse at Longford Bridge is another M & B house, and hereabouts there used to be an odd arrangement of canals. The present junction with the Oxford at Hawkesbury, still a mile distant, is the second such meeting of the two canals. Originally, when the Oxford arrived here in 1778, a dispute over tolls to be levied on traffic passing between the two waterways led to the Oxford being built to run alongside the Coventry, eventually to make the junction here. This circuitous state of affairs obtained until Hawkesbury as we know it today was opened in 1835. Even today, after all these years, the old course of the Oxford can be picked out just beyond the towpath.

Noise from the fiendishly busy M6 now becomes a problem; one that magically disappears as you walk under the bridge. Gone is the whoosh of traffic, replaced by the gentle clunk of concrete as slabs overhead move. Tended grass and moored boats now announce the approach to Hawkesbury Junction, one of the most evocative names in canal lore.

Here, at Sutton Stop as it was known to generations of boat people after the name of the first lock keeper, empty boats gathered to "await orders" - instructions on where to go and load. There are usually a couple of working boats to be found here which retail coal from their holds, maintaining a long tradition. The walk turns right, past another canal landmark, the Greyhound pub, and to the stop lock itself. The iron bridge spanning the junction was cast at Britannia Foundry, Derby, in 1837.

Across the water on the Coventry Canal are the remains of an old engine house that pumped water from local mines into the canal. The Newcomen Atmospheric Steam Pumping Engine once installed here is gone, fortunately preserved at Dartmouth Museum. Thomas Newcomen (1663-1729) was the chief begetter of practical steam power, living and working in that Devon town.

Hawkesbury Junction to Hawkesbury - ¹/₂ mile

This is the northern Oxford Canal. To the left, now private moorings, is where the idle narrowboats used to wait for work. A sharp right bend and the site of Coventry Power Station is reached. Although electricity is no longer generated, there is a huge collection of switchgear and overhead cables. The whole area crackles and fizzes most alarmingly in wet weather. After another 500 yards, leave the towpath at the Elephant and Castle, unusually, for this area, selling ales by Charles Wells, and you are back at your starting point.

WALK 21 - HINCKLEY TO NUNEATON - COVENTRY & ASHBY CANALS

These two Warwickshire towns almost join with each other, town centre to town centre by crow being less than 4 miles. Only the A5 trunk road keeps them apart. But by canal the journey is almost three times as long. The initial part of the walk is along the Coventry

Canal, details of which can be found in Walk 14.

From Marston Junction the way is along the Ashby Canal. Any history of canal carrying in this area of the Midlands would be incomplete without reference to this long and much neglected waterway. The Ashby Canal originally linked the Coventry Canal with the south Derbyshire collieries, giving access from the Moira area into the Midlands. The plans for arms to serve a whole range of collieries at the north end never came to pass, and coal was delivered canalside by a series of tramways which eventually covered the area. The northern 9 miles of canal have disappeared, the victim of subsidence.

But not for long. A substantial length is now under restoration, and it is hoped that the whole stretch will be back in water before too long. The rest of the Ashby is pretty, unspoilt, and generally well clear of habitation. It was originally constructed to barge (14ft) standards, as the aim was to link up with the River Trent. There are no locks on this canal, indeed, none at all on the walk. There was trade on the Ashby until the final days of working narrowboats, the last load leaving as recently as 1970.

The Warwickshire coalfield was centred around Bedworth, and colliery spoil heaps were an accepted part of the landscape here until fairly recent times. Now, they have mostly been graded into gentler hills, and are grassed over, their present charm belying their ugly past.

BEFORE YOU START

WALK DISTANCE:	8¼ miles (or 9 miles: see text)
MAP:	OS Landranger Series No 140
START:	The junction of Croft Road and Tomkinson Road, Nuneaton, close to Nuneaton Borough Football Club's ground
PUBLIC TRANSPORT	Nuneaton is on the intercity network, and National Coaches call in the town
STARTING GRID REF:	SP 351917
CAR PARKING:	Usually plenty of space in Tomkinson Road. Saturday afternoons during the soccer season can be a bit congested

TRANSPORT:	Frequent service to Nuneaton Bus Station. Change there for the service between Nuneaton town and Hinckley. This operated by Midland Red; details on 01788 535555
REFRESHMENT:	All services in both towns. Pubs en route
NEAREST TIC:	The Library, Church Street, Nuneaton, Warwickshire CV11 4DR - 01203 384027

THE WALK

Should you eschew the bus service into Nuneaton, cross over the canal to the small traffic island. Turn right into Queens Road which will eventually lead you into the pedestrianised town centre, from where signs to the bus station will be found. Walking time is about 15 minutes, and turns the original $8^{1}/_{4}$ mile walk into one of 9 miles.

In Hinckley, alight in Coventry Road, close to an industrial estate where the road crosses the canal. Gain the towpath and head south.

Hinckley to Burton Hastings -3 miles

At the start, this path is well kept and frequently used by the locals. Under the first bridge is the old Hinckley Arm on the left. Still used as private moorings, this 300 yards of water was once busy with trading boats delivering coal to the town, which has an industrial past longer than most towns in the area. A stocking machine was installed in a mill here way back in 1640.

A railway passes overhead, used only infrequently by trains, and the town is soon left behind. The canal crosses Sketchly Brook and rounds a corner to reveal the unusually named Lime Kilns Inn. The name, of course, is self-explanatory, and there was once a wharf here at which the working boats used to call.

The pub has a pleasant garden alongside the canal, is a popular mooring for boats in season, and serves good food with Marston's

beer. The downside is the frenetic pace of traffic roaring by on the A5 trunk road; strangely at odds with a tranquil canal scene.

As the towpath strides off into the countryside, the mayhem is soon forgotten and the surrounding district becomes one of gentle rurality. Farms are the only sign of habitation, although Burton Hastings will soon come into view, a pretty village atop a gently rising hillside, the church of St. Botolph's prominent.

Burton Hastings to Marston Junction - 3 miles

Bridges 9 and 8 cross the canal as it creeps around the foot of the hill. These are both Grade 2 listed, constructed about 1800 from local limestone. Towpath restoration has clearly been a recent activity; the edge is reconstructed with wooden piling, and dredged to backfill. From bridge 6 the towpath starts to deteriorate quite markedly, making progress difficult for much of the way, and virtually impassable for some 100 yards. One can only hope that the good work recently performed behind will be extended to this section soon.

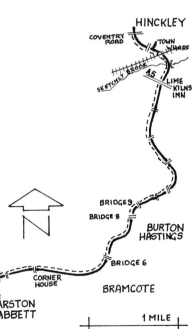

It is about this point that you realise that starting this walk without sturdy thorn- and nettle-proof trousers was not such a good idea! Brambles, blackthorn and nettles vie with each other to attack you first. It also makes you appreciate the sterling efforts of British Waterways on the section behind in cutting back hard on the blackthorn hedge which is now trying to close the gap between it and the water.

At bridge 5 there is refreshment at hand if wanted. Leave the canal, cross the road bridge, and

111

100 yards along is The Corner House, a friendly pub, also selling Marston's ales; a deservedly popular brew around these parts. The London to Glasgow electric railway rattles noisily overhead between bridges 4 and 3. The surrounding fields, somewhat of a wasteland, fall away to either side of the canal: subsidence, a sure sign that you are approaching a mining area.

Bridges 2 and 1 are built from Attleborough sandstone, as opposed to brick, and are also Grade 2 listed. Just before Marston Junction bridge is the site of a stop lock, now ungated. Originally built as a 14ft wide chamber, it was reconstructed to narrow dimensions in 1819. Although this meant that broad beam boats could not get beyond here, they still traded further back up the canal, linking the collieries with several wharves along the way. The junction between the two lines was not originally planned to be sited here, but along by the Griff Arm, a little further north.

Marston Junction to Nuneaton - 2¼ miles

A right turn sees the Ashby Canal left behind. To the left, only 3 miles away, is Hawkesbury Junction, and the Oxford Canal - see Walk 20. There was a maze of collieries between the two canal junctions, some of which actually had their own canal systems installed long before the Coventry arrived in 1769. When the "newcomer" was opened, they were linked in. The houses beyond the junction are part of Bedworth, now bereft of its pits.

There is little evidence around now to indicate its recent past, but at the apex of a sharp right-hand bend are the remains of the aforementioned Griff Arm. It's overgrown now, but still in water for about 400 yards or so until it meets a main road. From there it is infilled, although there is a public footpath along the old course should you wish to explore it. Griff Colliery was away to the right, in the direction of Arbury Park. Coal· was still loaded onto narrowboats on the Coventry Canal here until 1961 when the arm was closed.

Already, Nuneaton is starting to impose itself on the walk. There is a mixture of housing and industry on the towpath side, whilst across the way is a vast area of allotments, many of them still well tended and growing a splendid range of produce. At bridge number 21, Wash Lane, the walk ends. Leave the towpath and cross the canal to Tomkinson Road.

WALK 22 - POLESWORTH TO ATHERSTONE - COVENTRY CANAL

One of the shorter walks in this book, it passes through some pleasantly rural scenery and is always remote without any overpowering canal interest.

A brief look at the history of the Coventry Canal can be found in Walk 14 (p74).

BEFORE YOU START

WALK DISTANCE:	5 miles
MAP:	OS Landranger Series No 140
START:	Atherstone rail station
PUBLIC TRANSPORT:	As above. Atherstone is on the Trent Valley line from Rugby to Stafford. Nearest National Coach stop is Nuneaton
STARTING GRID REF:	SK 304979
CAR PARKING:	At the station
TRANSPORT:	Rail service to Polesworth. This is infrequent: the current timetable shows 4 a day, 3 on Saturdays and none on Sunday. Several companies operate an equally infrequent bus service. Details for these from Warwickshire Traveline - 01926 414140
REFRESHMENT:	Pubs and shops in Atherstone and Polesworth, nothing between
NEAREST TIC:	The Library, Church Street, Nuneaton, Warwickshire CV11 4DR - 01203 384027

Polesworth Train Station to Mill Bridge 53 - 1 mile

Leave the station platform, turn left and follow the road round to a T junction. Turn left, and immediately right at the main road. This runs through the middle of Polesworth, crossing over the River Anker to a crossroads. Walk straight across into Market Street. Travelling by bus, some stop outside the fire station here. Walk back to the crossroads and turn right into Market Street. A few yards along this road is canal bridge 53.

Mill Bridge 53 to Bradley Green Bridge 48 - 2 miles

Turn left onto the towpath and instantly the noise and hubbub of Polesworth disappear. The next bridge is a narrow road one with an ornate footpath added alongside.

Leaving the town behind, a gentle left bend and the line strides across the Anker valley, passing under the railway before turning sharp right. A small hillock and trees quickly turn this into an idyllic spot, the peace only disturbed by the occasional passage of a train.

As the canal narrows, on the opposite bank there can be seen the decaying remains of a swing bridge. Now well overgrown with bramble, it was in use within the memory of this writer. And what a pig it was! A very difficult battle needed to be fought with it before, reluctantly, movement was obtained.

The Anker is a constant companion on this walk, to a greater or lesser extent. Never far away,

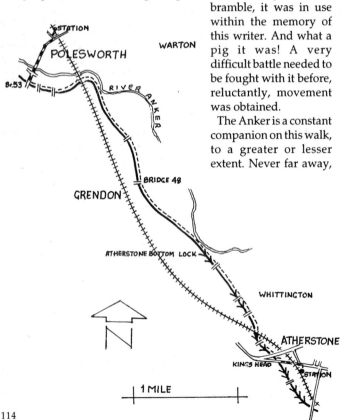

Grendon, Coventry Canal

it occasionally closes almost to the edge of the canal. The line itself is shelved into the valley side now for quite a long way. And it's delightfully remote with not the slightest hint of housing or any other living soul.

Flat but pretty agricultural land reveals Warton church spire visible on the skyline to the left.

Bradley Green Bridge 48 to Atherstone Train Station - 2 miles

Bridge 48 carries a quite busy minor road with the village of Grendon to the right. The towpath deteriorates for a few yards around this area, but is otherwise in excellent condition throughout the walk.

Moored boats occupy the far bank and beyond, the bottom lock of the Atherstone flight hoves into view. Eleven of them will lift the canal some 80ft. Still completely rural at this point, the main West Coast railway line is the only slight disturbance way off to the right. After the first two locks there is a longish pound broken by a pretty bridge, an iron platform with latticed sides on brick piers. Built as a footbridge, there is now no 'foot' to it, as the wooden footway has rotted and not been replaced.

To the right, atop the hill, is Merevale Hall. Built in the grounds of a ruined twelfth century abbey, this Tudor-like 'pile' was actually built in the early 1800s.

Locks come thick and fast. Bridge 46, and several to follow, have low arches so care is needed to avoid a sore head. Each one carries red and white paint to draw attention to the problem. Open field now give way to an altogether more wooded area, which in turn leads to the outskirts of Atherstone.

Once a facet of the Coventry Canal scenery, noted by the new A5 road crossing, is the allotment. Very much dying out around the country, they are still very strong in this area. There are more higher up the flight, and acres of them canalside in Nuneaton, on Walk 21. They almost seem to belong to another generation. This feeling is re-enforced by looking at the age of people tending them: how much longer will the concept survive?

The waterside pub here is the Kings Head, serving Davenports Ales. Just beyond, but before the bridge and lock 5, is a path to the left.* Take it, bear left at the road, pass under a 9ft high railway bridge and the station entrance is just beyond on the right.

These buildings were restored in the mid 1980s and won a First Class award from the Association of Railway Preservation Society in their Best Restored Station competition in 1985. It was presented by David Shepherd OBE, the well known artist and preserver of steam locomotives, and the guiding light behind the East Somerset preserved line at Cranmore.

---

* There is an alternative to finishing the walk here. It is possible to continue up the locks to the top and leave the canal to the left just beyond. This leads into the town. Turn left at the major road, and follow this down to the station.

WALK 23 - WOOTTON WAWEN TO STRATFORD-UPON-AVON - STRATFORD CANAL

That we have a walk along this canal at all is due to the enormous pressure placed on the Government by the Inland Waterways Association and other local bodies in the 1950s after the line had been listed for closure by the infamous Board of Survey in 1955.

The canal first reached Stratford-upon-Avon in 1816. It was built in two roughly equal sections. The northern part from the Worcester and Birmingham Canal at Kings Norton to Lapworth was completed in 1902. The heavily locked section to the south needed funds that were not available, hence the delay.

The concept of the canal was access to collieries in the Dudley area. Using the Dudley Number Two Canal from Selly Oak with the Worcester and Birmingham eliminated the expensive and congested canals around Birmingham city centre. Part of the Dudley Number Two is visited on Walk 29.

It was a successful undertaking initially, but suffered very early from railway competition. The directors sold out to the Great Western Railway in 1845. This caused severe dissent amongst the shareholders, and the deal was not finally concluded until 1856.

From then, it was the usual tale of neglect and indifference from the Great Western Railway. Traffic faded gently away, and the last recorded boat to reach Stratford was in 1935. The northern section was usable - just. Then came the first rumblings of the preservation movement. The swing bridge at Lifford Lane, near the junction with the Worcester and Birmingham, had been fixed. As a parliamentary Act authorising abandonment had not been obtained, the protesters pointed out that this was illegal and that they required passage. The bridge was replaced by a swing one.

Emboldened by this and other minor successes the movement had achieved, a major campaign to save the Stratford was launched. Because of the volume of protest after the announcement of closure, a Committee of Enquiry had to be established. At this time the then owners, the British Transport Commission, announced that bridge 59 at Wilmcote was to be lowered, removing navigational headroom. They also stated that it would cost £119,000 to close the canal. The protesters made the point that it would be much cheaper to restore, and their arguments won the day when on 22 May 1959 the Inspector found in their favour.

This proved to be the turning point in canal restoration. The cost benefit of restoration versus closure was established, and used to good effect, and many a mile of then feculent canal now owes its current restoration to that moment.

Later in 1959 the National Trust was persuaded to take responsibility for the lower section, and under the dynamic leadership of Denys Hutchins and his merry band of volunteers, who included service personnel and inhabitants of Her Majesty's Prisons, the restoration was completed at under half the cost of closure; the paradigm for many a subsequent project.

Queen Elizabeth the Queen Mother performed the official re-opening ceremony on 11 July 1964. The National Trust proved not to be the best people to look after the canal; with the best will in the world, it was not one of their stronger points. British Waterways took over on 1 April 1988, and maintenance is now carried out to their standards.

A silent vote of thanks to these early enthusiasts is called for here before enjoying the sylvan scenery on offer.

BEFORE YOU START

WALK DISTANCE:	7 miles
MAP:	OS Landranger Series No 151
START:	Stratford-upon-Avon town centre
PUBLIC TRANSPORT:	Rail and coach services into Stratford
STARTING GRID REF:	SP 204551
CAR PARKING:	There is a wide choice of available spaces except at the height of the tourist season
TRANSPORT:	Midland Red service X20 to Birmingham starts from outside MacDonalds, so you can nip in for a quick burger if the bus is not due! Enquiries on 0121 200 2700. There is also a good rail service between the two, but Wootton Wawen station is nearly a mile from the canal

REFRESHMENT:	See above. Everything you could hope for in Stratford, pub at Wootton Wawen and pubs and tea-room at Wilmcote, albeit not canalside
NEAREST TIC:	Bridgefoot, Stratford-upon-Avon, Warwickshire CV37 6GW - 01789 295262

THE WALK

Alight at Wootton Wawen and walk back towards the aqueduct. Just before reaching it turn left up the lane and first right. This brings you to the canal by bridge 53, but make sure that you allow yourself time to enjoy the village before you leave. It's a straggly sort of place but with a delightful collection of half-timbered houses, a superb church - St. Peters - and a fine Hall.

Wootton Wawan to Wilmcote - 3 miles

There are moored boats at first on the far side of the water, followed by the basin, home for an Anglo-Welsh hire fleet. The basin was originally cut when the canal's southward progress came to a halt here, the cause of that being just ahead - a delightful iron troughed aqueduct over the A34 trunk road. The towpath steps down, and with the water level at about chest height, passing boats take on an altogether different appearance.

The canal now holds the contour round a left-handed bend, and the towpath is almost level with the water here. Recent improvements have made walking a little less of a lottery; the wash from passing boats was always a threat.

A roving bridge located $1/4$ mile further takes the walk to the east side of the cut, where it remains until the last few yards in Stratford. This and subsequent bridges are all built from red brick which is now well weathered and appear thoroughly in keeping with their surroundings. The first lock on the walk follows next.

Called Odd Lock, it actually appears to be perfectly normal. Beyond is another aqueduct at Edstone. Identical in style to the one at Wootton Wawen, this one is about 200 yards long and takes the water over a river, the Birmingham to Stratford railway line, and a small country road.

A wooded section follows, the line weaving wildly. This is canal walking at its very best: a total absence of any sign of civilisation. Even the railway is well concealed although it is never more than a few yards away. The remnants of an old bridge by the winding hole on the outskirts of Wilmcote have one searching the map for "cse of old rly". But nothing is marked. It was actually an old tramroad that brought horse drawn waggons from nearby stone quarries down to the canal where it was loaded into boats.

The village of Wilmcote demands a break. It's around the halfway point, and has a couple of first class pubs. The whole place is delightful, but overrun with tourists, all heading for Mary Arden's cottage, Shakespeare's mother's home, which is open to visitors. Sitting in one of the pubs listening to the drinkers is probably what the Tower of Babel must have sounded like.

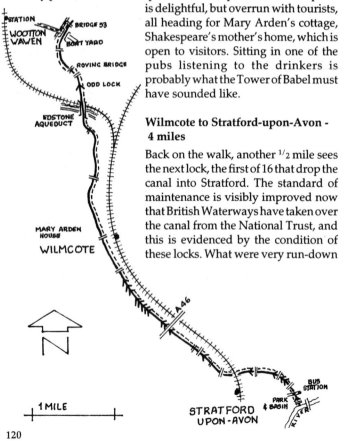

Wilmcote to Stratford-upon-Avon - 4 miles

Back on the walk, another $1/2$ mile sees the next lock, the first of 16 that drop the canal into Stratford. The standard of maintenance is visibly improved now that British Waterways have taken over the canal from the National Trust, and this is evidenced by the condition of these locks. What were very run-down affairs just a few years ago have changed almost beyond recognition.

At the bottom of the Wilmcote 11, the area to the left is now landscaped and planted with trees. Soon, visual evidence of the landfill site (corporation euphemism for rubbish tip) will be gone for ever. A new road bridge, red brick built and not too intrusive, signals the outer edge of Stratford-upon-Avon. And, regrettably, the canal seems to reach this beautiful town via the tradesmen's entrance. Factories, the gasworks, and a very low bridge bringing the railway over to the station all crowd around this point, although much of the old industry that was once serviced by the canal has now disappeared; replaced by rather twee housing. The first boats since Wootton Wawen are moored on the far side.

A roving bridge 68 takes the towpath back to the right-hand side. This has recently been rebricked and looks thoroughly in keeping with the area. Here the canal turns sharp right, and the resulting elbow seems to be the gathering place for the floating detritus that infests our urban canals these days.

The walk ends at the next bridge. From here to the river, some 100 yards, there is no towpath. Those who insist on reaching the canal's end must take their life in their hands and cross the road, which is eternally busy, leading into the park area opposite where there is a basin, the river lock and the junction.

Reprise:
One must be poor in spirit not to be able to appreciate the beauties of this town. And you do not need to be a Shakespeare lover. There are so many old buildings and pleasant riverside vistas that an extra hour or two in your schedule is a must.

If nothing else, hard by the end of the walk is a firm offering tours of the town on an open topped bus. Sightseeing sitting down. Perfect after a 7 mile walk.

Chapter 6:
The Birmingham Area

WALK 24 - LEABROOK TO WALSALL - WALSALL CANAL

This is the heart of the West Midlands. If leafy byways are your idea of perfect walking, this will disappoint. But if you have not yet sampled the pleasure of urban canals, cut your teeth on this one. Almost alone within this huge and often ugly conurbation, fascination with the history of a great transport system together with living remains make compelling walking. Approach it with an open mind and it will not disappoint. Parking problems in Walsall mean that this walk uses transport for the return leg.

The Walsall Canal is a constituent part of the Birmingham Canal Navigations. Their general history is detailed in Walk 25. The 7 mile Walsall line was opened in 1799 as an extension of the Wednesbury Canal at Ryders Green Junction and provided a through route to Birmingham. A one mile link from Walsall Junction to the Wyrley and Essington Canal at Birchalls Junction was opened in 1841. As with the rest of the Birmingham Canal Navigations, trade was heavy and, although a few branches off the canal were closed, most of it is as built almost two centuries ago.

BEFORE YOU START

WALK DISTANCE:	7½ miles
MAP:	OS Landranger Series No 139: The Geographers A to Z of Birmingham
START:	Leabrook Road, Wednesbury, on A461 Walsall to Dudley road
PUBLIC TRANSPORT:	Birmingham is the closest major point. Just about the only way you can't reach that city is by cruise liner! Dudley is closer, but without the range of services
STARTING GRID REF:	SO 977943

CAR PARKING:	Several side streets close by; Lea Avenue or Willingsworth Road nearest
TRANSPORT:	Centro bus 310 Walsall to Dudley via Wednesbury and Ocker Hill. Alternative frequent service to Wednesbury bus station leaving a ¹/₂ mile walk back to the start. Service details on 021 200 2700
REFRESHMENT:	Pub at start, several en route, everything you could need in Walsall
NEAREST TIC:	2 City Arcade, Birmingham, West Midlands B2 4TX - 0121 643 2514. 39 Churchill Precinct, Dudley, West Midlands DY1 7BL - 01384 250333

THE WALK

Walk down the hill to the canal bridge. The Bush, an M & B house, is canalside. Gain the towpath and turn left.

Leabrook to Moorcroft Junction - 1 mile

First impressions are of a relatively weed free canal with overgrown towpath, and that you are instantly into that little world of your own on a Birmingham Canal Navigations towpath. After 200 yards Wiggins Mill Bridge is reached. Cross to the right-hand side here, and the ¹/₂ mile long Gospel Oak Branch comes into view on the left. Opened in 1800 it was planned to link with Wednesbury Oak Loop, but the decision was taken to build at Bradley instead. It closed in 1954.

To the right are the remains of Leabrook Railway Basins. Owned by the Great Western Railway, a vast interchange of cargoes once took place here. Under the next (railway) bridge there used to be a canal crossroads, and the location of the sort of factories that made the name Birmingham synonymous with enterprise and industry throughout the world. Now, it's all gone. The Patent Shaft Steelworks was here, served by the Monway Arm.

But all is not lost. Recently, regeneration of this barren landscape has started. New industrial units are already in place, with much more promised. Before many years have passed, this walk will have taken on a very different aspect.

At the next bridge, Willingsworth Hall, is/was Moorcroft

Junction where the aforementioned Bradley branch was built. It climbed through 9 locks to come out close to British Waterways' Bradley Workshop. The first 1¼ miles opened in 1798 to serve Willingsworth Colliery, with the 1,000 yard extension to Bradley completed in 1849. The link was severed in 1961.

Moorcroft Junction to Walsall Junction - 5 miles

There now follows just a few yards with green trees lining the far bank before Moxley, more industry, houses, and several bridges over private arms. At the next bridge, on the left, is the Royal George pub, serving that most excellent of Midlands beers, Banks's. After the next bridge were two short arms on the left, both abandoned in 1953. There is still evidence of the Willenhall branch, but the Bilston, connected with a tramway, has disappeared completely. Darlaston

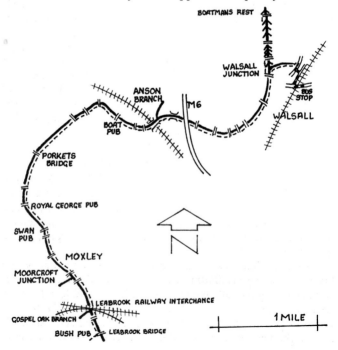

Comprehensive is on the right, a large school with playing fields.

The next bridge is Porkets, which has a different spelling on each of three maps. A new road, The Black Country Route, is now alongside the canal, changing the vista forever. This is Rough Hay, and looks to be well named. Houses circa 1920s/30s stand behind high fences. They appear to be in blocks of four and have small lean-to's, each with a chimney: built with their own individual wash-houses?

At Willenhall, factories on opposite sides of the canal used to be linked by an electrically operated bridge. Only the narrows remain, but it was extant as recently as 1982. At Bentley Bridge, more Banks's ale is available at the Boat. Bradley and Foster's old factory buildings line the left-hand bank here, whilst the towpath deteriorates markedly.

An aqueduct precedes the weeded remains of the Anson branch, which used to be over 2 miles long, also giving a connection with the Bentley Canal and the Wyrley and Essington. Crossing an embankment, the canal strides towards the M6, overlooking a nicely laid out (!) cemetery, where even gasholders have been prettified by painting them turquoise and blue in large diagonal panels. Beyond the motorway, an office block attached to the IMI works at James Bridge straddles the canal, and at Pleck are the remains of an old canalside warehouse with doors opening over the water and evidence of a hoist still to be seen.

Walsall Junction to Walsall via Walsall Top Lock - 1½ miles

On reaching the junction, cross to the left bank. The first lock is just beyond the junction, single gated in typical Birmingham Canal Navigations style. The water is very clear, and it is easy to see how many shopping trollies per mile this canal holds. Lock surrounds have been tidied up, turning a rather mundane section into something quite pleasing to the eye.

There are eight locks in the flight, and at the top a comely iron bridge with cast iron rails draws the eye, as does Birmingham Canal Navigations house 206, which was toll house and lock keeper's residence, whilst next door is the Boatman's Rest. Now the Birchills Canal Museum, it was built in 1900 by The Seamen's and Boatman's Society Midland District to provide boatmen with rest and relaxation not involving consumption of alcohol.

From here, turn round and walk back to the junction, cross the canal and turn left to follow the arm into Walsall. This really is the secret way into the heart of town. A well defined path eventually runs to the right of a recently redeveloped Walsall Basin and the end of the walk. Bear left into Park Street and at the bottom turn right into Bradford Street. The bus stand R is in Bradford Place, a few yards on the right.

WALK 25 - WOLVERHAMPTON TO MOXLEY - BIRMINGHAM CANAL NAVIGATIONS MAIN LINE, WEDNESBURY LOOP AND WALSALL CANAL

A walk through history could well describe the character of this walk. Looking at the canal as it is today, it needs a quantum leap of

Wolverhampton Top Lock

the imagination to try and recall a seething mass of working boats, horses, men and cargo; the whole scene overhung by a smoky sky. The Black Country was not so named without reason. This is often recalled in old photographs.

The history of inland navigation in England is encapsulated in the West Midlands system. The Birmingham Canal Navigations was a private company formed by the amalgamation of canal promoters and builders. It was extremely profitable, and at its height, a century ago, over 170 miles of canal were in use. The infrastructure was immense: 2,112 locks, 550 private arms, 3 very long tunnels; in fact, for almost a century, the Birmingham Canal Navigations was THE transport system in the West Midlands. A century ago well over 8 million tons of cargo moved along the water. Even in 1950 there were over 1 million tons.

Today there are around 112 miles of canal left: more than in Venice. And although the water is much cleaner, Gas Street Basin and the Oozells loop don't quite have the visual appeal of the Doges Palace or St. Mark's Square! Nevertheless, the system has its own fascination. Within a mile of central Birmingham it is possible to see kingfishers. Kestrels nest in disused factory walls, and the bloodcurdling howl of a dog fox is quite normal now. Flowers grow between the granite setts of the towpath and, in the midst of this teeming conurbation, people are few and far between.

A Birmingham Canal Navigations bridge is often made from cast iron, smartly painted in black and white. Not only do they span the water - they appear regularly along the towpath where once they crossed the entrance to private arms. The towpaths themselves are in fine condition throughout. Most of the canals are edged with brick, the result of years of labour by long gone craftsmen.

Here and there the local authorities have made an effort to improve the surrounds. This is particularly noticeable on Walk 27. Contrast that with this and the next walk. Using sections of infilled canal as links, it is possible to get right to the heart of this system. The Wednesbury Loop on this walk was the very first canal in place. Eventually, in 1772 it linked central Birmingham with the Staffordshire and Worcestershire Canal at Aldersley Junction - see Walk 16. James Brindley was the engineer responsible, and that meant a contour canal. At the time this was fine as there was simply no competition, but as trade burgeoned and the threat of railways was perceived, improvements were made.

Originally, there were 32 locks on the 22$^{1/2}$ mile canal. Smethwick locks were reduced from 12 to 6 in the 1790s by digging a cutting, and Thomas Telford was enlisted in the 1820s to shorten the route. This he did with bold cuttings and high embankments, producing essentially a straight line. In so doing, he took 7 miles off the journey between Wolverhampton and Birmingham.

After that, the main line through Wednesbury became a loop, still serving collieries. With their demise, much of the line became redundant and was closed south of Bradley in the 1950s. An indication of its tortuous nature can be found in that, by crow, from Broomfield Junction to Deepfields Junction on the main line is 1$^{1/4}$ miles. The Wednesbury line was 4$^{1/4}$ miles. That the northerly 1$^{1/4}$ miles remain is due to the fact that British Waterways' main engineering facility is located here.

BEFORE YOU START

WALK DISTANCE:	7 miles
MAP:	OS Landranger Series No 139
START:	Church Street, Moxley, the A41 Birmingham to Wolverhampton road
PUBLIC TRANSPORT:	Intercity rail and National Coaches both serve Wolverhampton and Birmingham. Local bus service forward
STARTING GRID REF:	SO 967959
CAR PARKING:	Side street only
TRANSPORT:	Centro service 79 operates along Holyhead Road to Wolverhampton bus station, just across the road from the canal. Service details on 0121 200 2700
REFRESHMENT:	All services in Wolverhampton, otherwise sparse waterside, but never too far away
NEAREST TIC:	18 Queens Square, Wolverhampton, West Midlands WV1 1TQ - 01902 312051

Walsall Top Lock (Walk 24)
The bonded warehouse at Stourbridge (Walk 29)

THE WALK

There is a bus shelter just beyond the traffic lights, heading towards Wolverhampton. Alight at the bus station and walk down towards the new road and the train station. A service road leads to the station, whilst a little to the left is Wednesfield road, a busy thoroughfare which passes over the canal and under the railway. On the left a pleasant area with seating overlooks the water. Walk through this to the canal and turn left, away from the lock. This is the same starting point as for Walk 16.

Wolverhampton to Deepfields Junction - 3 miles

The canal passes under a longish bridge before arriving at a large British Waterways warehouse. This was once used by Fellows, Morton and Clayton, a canal carrier from early days right up to nationalisation. There are traces of several private arms in the next 600 yards or so before the Wyrley and Essington Canal leaves to the left. The narrow section just off the main line was the site of a stop lock.

   An almost perfectly preserved basin - complete with canopy - beyond the junction was once a rail interchange point, of the LMS

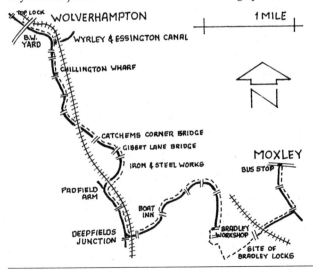

Railway variety. This is Chillington Wharf. The railway lines to the right were installed at a lower level so that cargo from boats could be transferred straight across. In August 1995, on the recommendation of English Heritage, this building became Grade II listed. Private arms come thick and fast now, with names leaping out from the history books. The Wulfruna Coal Company still use their wharf for storage of coal, but it no longer comes by boat.

An aura of calm now descends: that strange Birmingham Canal Navigations effect. All around is the throbbing heart of a great industrial conurbation, but the towpath is a place apart. A jogger, a dog-walker and a moorhen are the only living things in sight.

That Brindley was the progenitor of this canal is clear from the incessantly winding route. There are some delightfully named bridges now: Catchems Corner and Jibbet Lane (spelt with a G on some maps) are examples. Under the railway, a sharp left turn reveals a vast expanse of derelict land. This was once Stewarts and Lloyds iron and steel works at Bilston. Extensive arms served this area. Directly across the canal, another one reached towards an ironworks and linked by tramway to Parkfield colliery.

Deepfields Junction to Bradley Locks - 2 miles

At Deepfields Junction turn left into the Wednesbury Oak Loop. This is also the last point where moving boats are likely to be seen today. This dead-end is only on the route of those hardy souls who cruise the backwaters hoping to keep them open; their presence is vital to the retention of this sort of canal.

The towpath is of excellent quality, but the vast amount of weed reduces the canal to an ill-defined central channel, bearing mute testimony to the lack of use. Highfield Road bridge is a convenient place to break for refreshment. The Boat, alongside, serves an excellent pint of Hansons.

All too soon the end of this arm appears. British Waterways' Bradley Workshop is ahead, the source of all lock gates in the Midlands. Beyond, the line used to weave its way back to where the new cut joined at Bloomfields Junction, serving collieries and iron works along its way. The walk follows a path left of the works to a road. This is Bradley Lane; turn right, uphill, past the Old Bush Inn (Banks's fine ales). To the right, behind the pub's car park, the canal ends, and on the left a large brick built factory stands where boats once cruised. At the top of Bradley Lane turn left into Rose Street, which changes to Brierly Lane shortly. On the bend is a left turn which takes you into Peter Avenue, and 75 yards on the left is a gap just before the first house which leads behind the aforementioned brick building. A path follows the course of the canal along a high embankment.

Bradley Locks to Moxley - 2 miles

The path then turns left, downhill. On this manicured grass slope were the nine Bradley locks which lowered the canal 65ft to the Walsall level. The top six were built as recently as 1849, to provide another link to the Wolverhampton level. Towards the bottom, after what would have been lock 6, cross Great Bridge Road. Beyond there, the ground is unkempt, but a trickle of water flows along the old course. There is also some of the masonry associated with the locks to be seen. These were the originals, opened to Bradley Hall in 1798. The whole flight closed in 1961, but in recent years mutterings have emanated from the area that they might be rebuilt.

At the bottom of these remains there is water; badly silted and weeded, but still water. A footbridge combines with a huge pipe bridge to cross the Walsall Canal. Turn left and follow the Walsall Canal to Holyhead Road bridge, just over $^1/_2$ mile away, where the walk ends. This short section of the Walsall Canal is also used on Walk 24.

WALK 26 - TIPTON CIRCULAR - BIRMINGHAM CANAL NAVIGATIONS

A slight variation on the normal theme for this particular West Midlands perambulation: a proportion is not alongside water. It is still a canal walk within the meaning of the Act; it's just that one of the canals is closed. Closed but not disappeared, with much evidence of its existence still to be discovered. Over the years, the Birmingham Canal Navigations has lost some 60 of its original miles and a few bits of those lost waterways are included in this walk.

This fascinating amalgam of what used to be - and what still is

A footpath now cuts straight through an old lock on the Tipton and Toll End Communication Canal

- needs plenty of time. The desire to stop and draw mental pictures will happen frequently. As with any canal activity on the Birmingham Canal Navigations, green country vistas are in short supply, but that phenomenon, the Birmingham Canal Navigations Effect, is ever present. How is it possible to walk around the country's second city and manage to be so isolated?

A look at the Birmingham Canal Navigations as a whole can be found in Walk 25. For this walk, we will use the Old Main Line, the Gower Branch, the Wednesbury Old Canal, the Walsall Canal and the Toll End Communication Canal.

The Old Main Line is just that: the original course, reduced in status when Telford made his improvements. This also included the Gower Branch, built to link the two levels. The Wednesbury is a real antiquity. Opened in 1769, it survives today as the link between the New Main and the Walsall. The length beyond is now known as the Ridgeacre Branch, and has been truncated over the years, most recently in 1994 when the furthest $1/2$ mile was lost to road development.

The Walsall provides the third major Midlands canal level, at 408ft above sea level. It is only 8$^{1/2}$ miles in length, but became a vital piece in the Birmingham Canal Navigations jigsaw, linking the Wyrley and Essington in the north with the Birmingham line.

The Toll End Communication Canal is the missing link, provided to link Walsall with Dudley. It started life as a small branch off the Walsall in 1783 and bits were added over the years before the 3$^{1/2}$ mile line was completed in 1809. The (western) Tipton Green section closed in 1960, the rest in 1967.

BEFORE YOU START

WALK DISTANCE:	7$^{1/2}$ miles
MAP:	OS Landranger Series No 139
START:	Dolton Way, off Factory Road, Bloomfield. This leaves the A4037 Dudley to Wednesbury Oak road close to the canal bridge
PUBLIC TRANSPORT:	Tipton station on the Wolverhampton to Birmingham line is nearest. National Coaches serve both these
STARTING GRID REF:	SO 952927
CAR PARKING:	Dolton Way is a cul-de-sac holding a small industrial estate. Park in the farthest corner
TRANSPORT:	Not needed
REFRESHMENT:	Pubs, shops, cafes and fast food are never far away, but see footnote
NEAREST TIC:	39 Churchill Precinct, Dudley, West Midlands DY2 7BL - 01384 250333

THE WALK

A gate gives access to the canal towpath by the middle of the three Factory Locks on the New Main Line from Birmingham to Wolverhampton.

Factory Locks to Tividale Aqueduct - 2 miles

Turn left heading towards Birmingham. Just by Tipton station, the path crosses over a bridge which originally spanned the Three

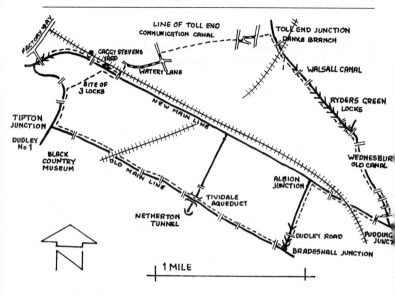

Furnaces Branch. Built to service ironworks beyond the railway, it has been infilled for many years. A pair of bridges give a view into Alan (Caggy) Stevens yard with its jumble of boats: some old, some new. The second bridge carries a plaque informing you that this was Watery Lane Junction, where the Toll End Communication crossed the main line. Across, a path between the houses clearly defines the course; and the walk. It was the arrival of Mr. Telford's work that made the junction.

Cross the main line by the next bridge which is a few yards further along and walk back to the junction. Turn left and follow the footpath. There were three locks in Tipton Green flight, which took the canal up 20ft to the Wolverhampton level. The site of the bottom and top locks can only be identified by a ridge in the ground, but the middle one is partially intact, with the footpath running through the centre of the chamber. It is even possible to tell that the bottom gate was of the single, Birmingham Canal Navigations type. At the top of the rise is the Old Main Line. Turn left. For reference, a green roofed building with a large centre arch across the water is a toilet.

The statue in this small park commemorates one William Perry, a boatman who achieved a sort of fame in the last century. Known as Bill, the Tipton Slasher, he was boxing Champion of England from 1850 to 1857 before returning to the 'cut' to resume his original calling.

Under the first road bridge is a house with its cast Birmingham Canal Navigations number plate - 100 - plainly visible. Beyond is Tipton Junction. Here, the Dudley Number 1 Canal - see Walk 29 - diverges. The narrow entrance was the site of a stop lock.

Around the corner, across the water was a line built by Lord Ward before the tunnel opened. Infilled at this end, it has been excavated within the Black Country Museum site which lies just beyond.

The canalside houses of David Avenue, Dudley, back onto the canal here but, with one possible exception, follow the lead of local industry by showing a very firm back to the water. High fences, corrugated iron and old pallets mingle with rubbish to present a particularly sad and dreary section of canal. Later on, after a disused steelworks tip, there is some very pleasant housing under construction with paved areas to the water's edge and mooring rings. Beyond the road bridge is a more varied development, but set back from the canal somewhat. No problem: construct an arm and a basin and bring the water to the door!

At Tividale, the Old Line crosses the New Line on an aqueduct as the latter plunges into the Stygian blackness of Netherton tunnel. The toll island and Birmingham Canal Navigations houses are still extant.

Tividale Aqueduct to Pudding Green Junction - 2 miles

By the time Bradeshall Junction is reached, the towpath has passed over two more bridges that once spanned private arms. At the junction, cross the branch and turn left. The staircase lock here is the only one on the Birmingham Canal Navigations. Be careful as you reach the bridge under Dudley Road as it's very low.

At the end of this branch is Albion Junction. Join the New Main Line. Across from the junction is a concrete capping. This was where the Dunkirk Branch left, passed under the railway, and ran for a short distance along an embankment. It was abandoned not long after the last war.

Turn right now, and just before the railway passes overhead, there was another crossroads (or should it be crosswaters?). The extension beyond the railway was only a very short affair, but the section to the right - the Roway Branch - used to form yet another crossroads a few hundred yards further on as it headed north to join the Wednesbury Old. These junctions were formed when the New Line swept through here in 1826. All trace of the Roway appears to be obliterated.

Use the next bridge, Oldbury Road, as a roving bridge, and cross to the other side of the canal. Just beyond is Pudding Green Junction.

Pudding Green Junction to Toll End Junction - 1½ miles

Turn left here. This also was a crossroads. On the opposite bank Izon Old Turn, now long gone, was the original course of the Wednesbury Canal before the New Main Line arrived.

After only a few yards, a roving bridge takes the path to the left-hand side. Here, the junction of the northern end of the Roway Branch can still be seen. Keep to the left as the Wednesbury Old veers off to the right, and the first canalside pub is reached. The six Ryders Green locks lower the canal to the Walsall Level. Here, there are several old canals. To the left, at the very tail of the bottom lock, was the start of Haines Branch; a factory now occupies the site. This once busy branch served several collieries, and had its own series of short branches.

The mass of waste ground to the right was Great Bridge interchange basin where canal originated traffic was transferred into LMS Railway wagons for wider distribution. This was a particular feature of the Birmingham Canal Navigations with examples all over the system. They also helped to keep traffic on the water long after other areas had abandoned it.

On the right, beyond the railway, lay the Danks Branch. The land here is in the process of being reclaimed, and the line is difficult to trace, but, again, a railway crossing is the pointer. Incidentally, the road bridge here carries cast metal plates with the legend MDCCCXXV.

A pipe bridge, close to a new factory, is the only evidence now of the location of Toll End Junction.

Toll End Junction to Factory Locks - 2 miles

This is the eastern end of the Tipton Green and Toll End Communication Canal. Turn left and walk beside the railings, which was the course of the canal. Ahead, Toll End Road bridge is still plain to see, and standing on it, the route can be discerned, curving away left. At this road turn left, and after a few yards turn right into Harrold Street.

At the end bear right into Aston Street and cross the main road, Bridge Street, onto the grassed area. It is then possible to pick up the line at the right-hand side. Through the gate, the raised ground indicates the site of one of the locks. Take the centre path through trees, and aim for the tower at the far end of the park. Standing just to the right of this is another bridge which, again, gives you the course.

Leave the park by the right-hand path, and across the road is Upper Church Lane Community Park. The canal used to arrive from the left in a sharp bend, pass though lock 4 (the rise in the ground) and form a junction in the right-hand corner. Left used to make for the New Main Line, whilst a short arm to Cotterill Farm colliery cut back across the road. What a place to stand awhile and let the imagination run riot.

Leave the park and turn right past the commercial premises now standing empty. Inside their entrance gate at the far side was the site of lock 5. It was filled in and levelled to form a car park for the company's employees. Now all gone. It's a sobering thought that one day an industrial archaeologist will painstakingly remove the infill here and marvel at eighteenth century man's transport system.

At the traffic island turn right along Alexandra Road. The gradient steepens and the road curves as it crosses the old course. Here, on the left, is an unmade road, Watery Lane. Walk up here, pausing at the gate of a plant hire company to locate the railway bridge over the course. Cross the railway through the wicket gates, regain the towpath of the main line and turn right for the short walk back to Factory Locks.

Note: A couple of hundred yards off the walk in Tipton is one of the lesser known attraction of this area. Mad O'Rourkes Pie Factory is a pub, taken over from a brewery chain. No effort is spared to recreate the atmosphere of a generation ago.

Dummy hams hang from ceiling rails, earthenware pudding basins decorate, along with blue and white patterned ceramic tiles. They even sprinkle a little sawdust on the floor. Beer is excellent, locally brewed by a very small brewery, but, if you visit, do the walk first; then you will have an appetite to tackle the food! This is simply superb in its presentation and originality, with quality not far behind. Desperate Dan's Cow Pie is almost as big as the one the comic character used to tackle: meat, potato and vegetables all under one crust, and horns as well! Fancy something different? Is there anywhere else in the world you can get Black Pudding Thermidor?

WALK 27 - BIRMINGHAM AND FARMERS BRIDGE CIRCULAR - BIRMINGHAM CANAL NAVIGATIONS

A microcosm of canal history. What better way to describe this walk around the centre of Birmingham. With hardly a blade of grass to be seen, this is a walk through the industrial heartland of England packed to overflowing with interest, whilst isolated from the frenetic pace of the country's second city in a way that will amaze non-BCN aficionados. There are no Elysian fields, stark hills or delightful vistas: just pure history. It's also a circular walk, removing the need for return transport.

Although the last mile or so uses the same length of canal as the outward section, do not be deterred. It's quite amazing how different things will look.

It is also the first of a staggering 49 locks that litter this walk. Birmingham may seem a fairly flat city, but try telling that to a boater. First of all, he will have climbed to what is known as the Birmingham level at 453ft above sea level. Then, another three locks reach the Wolverhampton level, 473ft, whilst the Titford Canal in West Bromwich reaches 511ft, the highest usable canal in the country. This is higher than the Llangollen Canal in the Welsh mountains; even higher than the Leeds and Liverpool that actually crosses the Pennines.

BEFORE YOU START

WALK DISTANCE: 9 miles
MAP: OS Landranger Series No 139

The Farmers Bridge lock flight on the BCN

START:	Gas Street, Birmingham. This lies to the right of the A456 Halesowen to Birmingham road just after the Five Ways flyover and before the Convention Centre on the left
PUBLIC TRANSPORT:	Digbeth Road coach station and New Street train station are a few minutes' walk away
STARTING GRID REF:	SP 063867
CAR PARKING:	Metered (except Sundays) on surrounding streets
TRANSPORT:	Not needed
REFRESHMENT:	Surprisingly, very little. The canal tends to be shut off from the road, and although pubs and shops can be seen, they are generally inaccessible
NEAREST TIC:	2 City Arcade, Birmingham, West Midlands B2 4TX - 0121 643 2514

THE WALK

Join the canal through a small archway in the wall and down a well worn path. Where else but Worcester Bar - better known as Gas Street Basin. What an evocative name in canal circles: yet a place that has changed so much over the last decade as to be unrecognisable. For better or worse is a subjective opinion that probably has much to do with one's age. Once, the area was almost completely cut off from the world, with only a tiny fraction of locals knowing of its existence. In front are the few old working boats still managing to give some character to the area. Beyond is a pub, hotel and offices: all shining new, not yet ingrained with Birmingham grime. The footbridge, a reasonable facsimile of Birmingham Canal Navigations bridges, is also new, replacing a ground level swing bridge which was adequate when only boat people used the centre island, the infamous Worcester Bar.

When the Worcester and Birmingham Canal obtained their Act in 1791, the Birmingham Canal Navigations, fearing loss of both trade and water, would not allow a connection with their system. It was written into the Act that they were not allowed to come within 7ft of the Birmingham Canal Company's water. This meant that traffic between the two canals was unloaded at one side and trans-

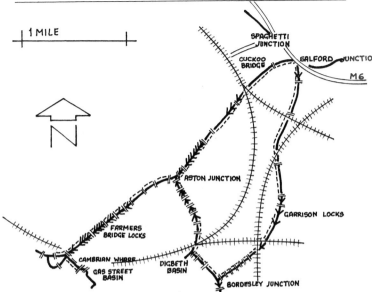

shipped to the other company's boats.

By 1815 wiser counsels had prevailed, and a new Act was obtained to link the systems via a stop lock. This explains the narrows. Here lock gates were fitted so that boats could not make a physical connection without stopping to pay their dues.

A closer look at the Worcester and Birmingham Canal will be found in Walk 30, whilst the Birmingham Canal Navigations story is told in Walk 25.

Gas Street Basin to Aston Junction - 1½ miles

Turn left and head towards yet another area of complete change. Gone are the factories, the myriad changes of headroom under Broad Street bridge, which used to be longer than some tunnels, and the air of dereliction. Now it's vibrant, populated by well heeled visitors sporting identity badges from the Birmingham International Convention Centre.

Old Turn Junction; a crossroads (or crosswaters) and more redevelopment. The vast bulk of the National Indoor Arena now dominates where smoke blackened brick stood before. There are also people. Cross the Oozells Street loop which was the original contour canal built by James Brindley. Now, with no towpath, it is for boats only.

Ahead is the "New" Main Line, Telford's reconstruction that shortened the trip to Wolverhampton by several miles (and hours). Beyond the junction, cross the New Main Line by the footbridge, turn right, left at the Junction, and a few yards brings you to the top of Farmers Bridge locks. Cambrian Wharf opposite is the truncated remains of the Newhall branch. The row of cottages to the right of the Long Boat pub were ex BCN on Kingston Row. They still carry the old system of numbering. In the 1970s when this area was redeveloped, British Waterways used to have a gift shop here, but it has long since gone.

There is a toll booth by the top lock. Here, boats were gauged to discover their weight and tolls levied accordingly. The Birmingham Canal Navigations was littered with these pretty buildings. Now they have all virtually disappeared; as did this one - almost - in 1991. Excavation work close to the site was the probable reason for its sudden and total collapse, the current building being a carefully rebuilt replica.

This area has given more than its fair share of grief to the British Waterways maintenance people in recent years. Opposite, and just below the lock, the retaining wall was the scene of a spectacular blow-out in the late 1980s, closing the flight for a long time. A large section of the wall just disintegrated and a huge cascade of water rapidly drained the canal above.

Down the flight, British Waterways have made a concerted effort to prettify the path and surrounds. And generally succeeded, apart from the incongruity of traditional style cast iron fingerposts giving metric distances. Strategically located wall plaques give an insight into the history of the area, and the way the flight used to operate.

Already, after half a dozen locks, the canal becomes more private. The concrete canyon with the BT tower overhead is awesome, whilst the ingenious elongated side ponds, vital to maintain a head of water for this busy flight, seem to (and do) belong to another age. The iron footbridge over a private arm by a museum was once the

300 yards long Whitmore Arm. In this area of tranquillity, it's almost impossible to imagine the frenetic boating activity here day and night. That night working was vital is evidenced by the remains of gas lighting fixed to the walls. There were over a hundred wharves and factories between the top lock and Aston Junction alone.

The brick bridge over the bottom lock of this flight is the old Great Western Railway entrance to Snow Hill station. Closed years ago as a result of the Beeching Report of the 1960s, it is now enjoying a renaissance as rail becomes an ever more important part of the transport strategy of this city.

Beyond is ¹⁄₂ mile of lock free walking, adorned by a couple of the Horsley black and white painted iron bridges that make any journey in this area such an aesthetically satisfying experience.

Aston Junction to Bordesley Junction - 1¹⁄₂ miles

At Aston Junction turn right, across the canal, and take the Digbeth branch. Once again, most of the buildings that housed factories have been swept away, replaced by modern, generally attractive small factory units. Beyond the short Ashted tunnel is a flight of six locks leading to Digbeth Basin. Once a hive of boating activity, this area is in the early stages of rejuvenation. Given another few years, the boatmen of the 1960s will have great difficulty in recognising a single landscape either here, or anywhere on this walk.

Bordesley Junction to Salford Junction - 2¹⁄₂ miles

Except for Bordesley Junction, that is: still remote, and away from the more popular cruising routes. Off to the right are the Camp Hill locks and the Grand Union Canal to London, whilst the walk turns left to the Saltley Cut - the Birmingham and Warwick Junction Canal to use its Sunday name. A relative newcomer, opened in 1844 to link with the Tame Valley Canal, it was instantly crowded with trade. This is surely the most evocative section of the whole walk. Along here used to be the Fellows Morton Clayton boat dock, arms to the Birmingham gasworks, exchange sidings with the LMS Railway, Midland Tar Distillers, power station basins, to list only a few. Now much of it is a barren waste, awaiting the hand of the redeveloper.

Along this section lies a flight of five locks. It's also as close as the walk comes to housing. Approaching the Gravelly Hills interchange (Spaghetti Junction, if you prefer) with the M6 and its associated linking roads, Nechells Shallow lock is passed. Before this road system was even a nightmare in the planner's mind, Salford Junction was the canal's own multi-junction. Now, underneath the mayhem, only the occasional jogger and dog-walker offer company. It's also remarkably quiet; at least, allowing for what is going on overhead.

Salford Junction to Aston Junction - 2 miles

Turn left, and left again towards the Aston flight of locks. The line disappearing off under the motorway is the Tame Valley Canal. This was another late-comer, opening in 1844, virtually the last narrow canal constructed in England. Its purpose was to allow traffic for the Wolverhampton direction a speedier passage, and to avoid the heavily congested Farmers Bridge flight. It links with the Walsall Canal at Tame Valley Junction, part of Walk 26. Its late arrival on the canal scene is evidenced by a straight wide line that carves through hills in cuttings, and over valleys on embankments. It also crosses the M5 motorway on a concrete aqueduct, just before that road meets the M6.

The River Tame runs below everything here, crossed by the canals on aqueducts. A short lock-free pound takes the canal through more industrial dereliction, with hardly a human shape to be seen, and towards the bottom lock of the Aston flight of eleven. Before long, there is some really dramatic redevelopment: new offices, shops, and businesses. In fact a whole area of old Birmingham has been flattened, transforming what was before with some tasteful work. The towpath is improved, and across the canal a delightful fountain plays adjacent to a model lock; as if there weren't enough of the real ones about!

Aston Junction to Gas Street Basin - 1¹/₂ miles

At the top of the flight you are back at Aston Junction. Retrace your steps to Gas Street, and marvel at another canal phenomenon: everything looks completely different on a return journey. This is particularly so as the canal sneaks up on the Post Office tower, almost passing directly below it. Just one more aspect of this walk that is so totally fascinating.

Chapter 7:
Worcestershire

WALK 28 - KIDDERMINSTER TO STOURPORT-ON-SEVERN - STAFFORDSHIRE AND WORCESTERSHIRE CANAL

As one of the earlier English canals, its gestation and birth were largely untroubled. It was another part of the "grand plan" to link the rivers Mersey, Humber and Severn. The start followed hard on the heels of the Trent and Mersey, but, with the major engineering works needed on that line, the Staffordshire and Worcestershire opened first.

46 miles and 43 locks linked the Trent and Mersey with the River Severn at a place that was to become Stourport. Within months of the canal's opening, The Birmingham Company completed their link at Aldersley - see Walk 16 - linking Birmingham and Bristol by water for the very first time.

Trade burgeoned in those heady early days. Fired with success the company invested in the Thames and Severn Canal - see this author's *Canal Walks - South* - to provide a direct, if somewhat circuitous route from the Midlands to London. The opening of the Oxford Canal, followed later by the Grand Junction, saw any hope of profit from that venture disappear in smoke. But traffic, boosted by the opening of the Stourbridge and Dudley canals in 1792, continued to ensure a handsome profit for the shareholders.

But clouds were starting to build. The Severn could be difficult to navigate in either drought or flood, and improvements were badly needed. Then the Worcester and Birmingham Canal became a reality in 1815, having taken an incredible 22 years to complete. This made an easier - and shorter - passage to Worcester, a fact compounded by construction of the Dudley Number Two Canal which linked to the Worcester and Birmingham at Selly Oak and channelled huge tonnages of traffic away from the Staffordshire and Worcestershire.

Railways - of course - affected traffic, but the canal still held on to much of its local coal trade. This ensured that it was possible to pay a dividend right up to nationalisation in 1948. The then new owners, the British Transport Commission, had scant regard for canals as a means of transport, and no investment or encouragement was forthcoming. Thus, the last regular commercial trade disappeared in the late 1950s, and plans were floated for closure.

This drew howls of protest locally, as the leisure potential was beginning to be discovered. A Society was formed who stalled the proposals whilst larger - national - forces were marshalled, and the plan defeated.

Today, there remains a fine canal, much of it exceedingly pretty. Sadly, the prettiest sections also have a paucity of public transport, making it difficult to access. But each end is covered in this book; on this and Walk 13. A third, brief, visit is made on Walk 16, giving an acceptable flavour of the whole.

BEFORE YOU START

WALK DISTANCE:	4^1/$_2$ miles
MAP:	OS Landranger Series No 138
START:	York Street, Stourport-on-Severn
PUBLIC TRANSPORT:	Rail and coach services to Kidderminster
STARTING GRID REF:	SO 812712
CAR PARKING:	Side roads close to Stourport Basin
TRANSPORT:	Midland Red West Services 11, 12 13, 13A, 14, 15, 15A 16 and 293 all go to Kidderminster, but none operates on Sundays. Full details on 01905 763888
REFRESHMENT:	Everything at each end, plenty of pubs between
NEAREST TIC:	Severn Valley Railway Station, Comberton Hill, Kidderminster, Worcestershire DY10 1QX - 01562 829400

THE WALK

In Stourport, walk along York Street and take the first right. The bus leaves from outside the post office. Get off in Kidderminster bus station and walk back the way the bus came in. On reaching the first main road, turn right along New Road and 100 yards along, at the traffic lights, turn right into Castle Road. Walk over the river and, with Knight's Variety Club on the left, a wide entrance opposite gives access to the towpath.

Castle Road Bridge to Pratts Wharf - 2¹/₂ miles

Turn left and pass under the bridge: and take a warning that will apply at several bridges along this canal. The arches tend to be of a very gentle curve which means that where the curving platform meets the parapet, there is often restricted headroom. Note also the large cast plate attached to the abutment. This was the individualistic style of the Staffordshire and Worcestershire who fitted these. They carry both name and number. Sadly, over the years they have become collector's items, and most of the originals have been stolen. The replacements, secured in a way to make them almost impossible to remove, are accurate copies, but lack the aged and corroded appeal of the originals.

The walk initially is through the factory area of the town, but this does not last for long. A bright new pub, The Watermill, and a busy road bridge mark the end of Kidderminster and the start of the rural section that will last to Stourport.

Around a bend, with the canal cut into the side of a sandstone outcrop,

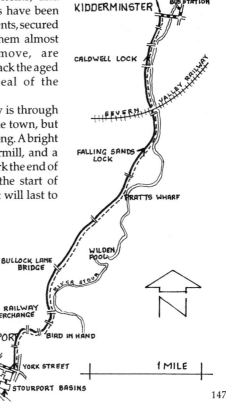

KIDDERMINSTER
BUS STATION
CALDWELL LOCK
SEVERN VALLEY RAILWAY
FALLING SANDS LOCK
PRATTS WHARF
WILDEN POOL
BULLOCK LANE BRIDGE
RIVER STOUR
OLD RAILWAY INTERCHANGE
STOURPORT
BIRD IN HAND
BUS STOP
YORK STREET
RIVER
STOURPORT BASINS

N

1 MILE

the first lock comes into view. Caldwell lock has only a shallow fall, but the overhanging trees and the rock outcrop make it very picturesque. Note too the gap in the centre of the bridge platform below the lock. This was to allow the towline between boat and horse to pass without being disconnected. A similar idea is used on the Stratford Canal, as will be seen in the course of Walks 18 and 23.

The next bridge is a grand affair, made from brick and very tall. It carries the Severn Valley Railway on its way to Kidderminster. This was one of the private railway companies formed in the 1960s in the death throes of British Railways steam. This was an ex-Great Western Railway branch line that, ironically, was one of the early recipients of the GWR experiment with lightweight diesel railcars. After closure a preservation society was formed that today operates one of the premier steam lines in the country.

Operating from Bridgnorth in Shropshire, the line follows a generally southerly course alongside the River Severn. For many years the line only ran to Hampton Loade, but subsequent developments have seen the remainder of the original line opened. It now continues before turning east, crossing the river just below Bewdley and running into the side of Kidderminster main line station. Although a Great Western Railway line, there is ample evidence of locomotives from other railway companies, together with a fine collection of preserved diesels.

Its time-capsule effects are much prized by film companies who regularly shoot scenes there. One notable one was the remake of John Buchan's *The Thirty-Nine Steps*, starring Robert Powell. A sequence that has our hero swinging from the train over a bridge was taken a few miles north of Kidderminster. But, astonishingly, the film company had the train pulled by a locomotive built in the late 1940s for action prior to the 1914-18 war!

Falling Sands lock follows, and beyond, a fine iron towpath bridge - very similar to ones seen on walks around the Birmingham Canal Navigations - takes the walk over an old arm. Here, the remains of a lock can be clearly identified. This was Pratts Wharf, and connected the canal with the River Stour which comes close at this point. The river was navigable for almost a mile downstream where it served an ironworks, built in the mid-1840s. The river was navigable for almost a mile downstream where it served an

Park-like setting for locks at Stourport-on-Severn, Staffs and Worcester Canal

ironworks, built in the mid 1980's. The river was in use until after the last war. Now it is unnavigable.

Pratts Wharf to Stourport Basin - 2 miles

Continuing along the tree-lined Stour valley, the canal holds something of a straight course now for the next mile or so, until the outskirts of Stourport come into view. There is also a derelict railway bridge. This used to meet the steam line near Bewdley, but has not been restored. There is a long arm to the right which used to be an interchange basin where rail freight was moved to boat for final delivery. Unusual, this, for most interchanges over the years saw traffic passing the other way. Much of the iron and coal that travelled through Pratts Wharf and down the Stour originated here. A large capstan-like construction on the towpath was used to winch boats in and out of the arm.

At the following bridge, the Bird in Hand pub offers Whitbread Ales and food, and if you need a small shop, the track away to the left will produce one some 50 yards along. The row of cottages alongside the path beyond the pub were canal houses, built around 1800. This signifies the start of Stourport proper now, although the canal still has one last mighty convulsion around the sandstone before finally heading for town. By the prettily rebuilt footpath, the Rising Sun sells Banks's Best Midlands ale, and there is a chip shop, supermarket, and most of the other needs on a walk of this kind.

The expanse of dead land on the far bank approaching the next lock used to be the company maintenance yard, but in more recent times was a hire fleet base. The lock is York Road, and it drops the canal into the expanse of Stourport Basin. The car parking streets are to the left, but an exploration of the old basins is almost mandatory.

There are four of them, not all easily accessible on foot. Cross the road and continue down Mart Lane and turn right around the rear of the pub. There will be discovered the broad locks which originally connected basins to river. A little further along, towards the funfair, a flight of narrow staircase locks will be seen. These were an afterthought, not constructed until some ten years after the canal had opened.

WALK 29 - NETHERTON TO STOURBRIDGE - DUDLEY NO 1, DUDLEY NO 2 & STOURBRIDGE CANALS

A study of maps before setting out on this walk may give the impression that you are walking through some of the worst parts of the once notorious Black Country. Not a bit of it. Although the adjective "beautiful" could never be used, it's full of interest and offers a remarkable degree of solitude.

The Dudley canals in this area are part of the Birmingham Canal Navigations. A look at the overall effect of this system will be found in Walk 25. The Number 1 Canal linked the Wolverhampton to Birmingham main line at Tipton Junction with the Stourbridge Canal, giving a shorter route to the River Severn.

The Number 2 line left the Number 1 at Park Head Junction and ran east to join the Worcester and Birmingham Canal, then under construction, at Selly Oak.

The opening of these two canals saw the Dudley company constantly at odds with the Birmingham Canal Navigations. The latter had a monopoly of trade to the Severn via the Wolverhampton locks - see Walk 16 - and their refusal to countenance a direct link in Gas Street - on Walk 27 - worked against them when freight was able to reach the southern end of the conurbation without the need to use their water.

However, there was a natural barrier to the completion of the Number 2. A tunnel at Lappal was needed: all 3,795 yards of it. The geology of this region was such that the whole area was very unstable, creating a tunnel that was claustrophobically low and narrow. Passage was so difficult that a pump was installed at the western portal. This delightfully Heath Robinson idea actually worked. A gate in the canal was closed and water pumped into the tunnel, effectively flushing an eastbound boat through. When a westbound passage was needed, the gate was opened, and the higher level already created by pumping ran back through the tunnel, dragging the boat with it. With a headroom of just 6ft and a couple of inches either side of the boat, the opportunity to get through much more quickly must have been manna from heaven for the boatmen.

Subsidence and instability were a constant drain on the company purse, and frequent closures did not help. This expenditure kept the company in a parlous financial position, and in 1846 it became part of the Birmingham Canal Navigations. Eventually, in 1917 part of the tunnel collapsed. This was the final straw, and the canal from there to Selly Oak was abandoned.

The history of the Stourbridge Canal is intertwined with that of the Dudley. They had an end-on connection at Delph and traffic passing along one invariably used the other. But, despite this close liaison, they were never united financially, and the Stourbridge retained its independence until nationalisation in 1948.

But by this time trade was disappearing and by the late 1950s the line was only passable with difficulty. There then occurred one of the first major successes of the restoration movement. To draw attention to the state of this canal, the Inland Waterways Association scheduled its National Rally for the canal in 1962. British Waterways were determined that the canal would be abandoned and attempted to stop the rally. This act, of doubtful legality, failed and 118 boats struggled through to the site. Faced with determination of this nature, and certain that any attempt to have the canal legally abandoned would be thwarted, British Waterways agreed that the Staffordshire and Worcestershire Canal Society could attempt restoration. Their volunteers and funds, combined with British

Waterways know-how, restored the lock flight, and the canal was navigable again by 1967.

BEFORE YOU START

WALK DISTANCE:	9 miles
MAP:	OS Landranger Series No 139
START:	The Bonded Warehouse, Stourbridge Basin, on the A491 road from Stourbridge to Wolverhampton
PUBLIC TRANSPORT:	Rail service to town. Dudley is the nearest large town for coach travellers
STARTING GRID REF:	SO 899848
CAR PARKING:	Side streets in the area
TRANSPORT:	Midland Red service 248 to Dudley. Service information on 0121 200 2700
REFRESHMENT:	Pubs and shops either canalside or close by occur frequently
NEAREST TIC:	Traveller Joy, 47 High Street, Kinver, West Midlands DY7 6HE - 01384 872940 or 39 Churchill Precinct, Dudley, West Midlands DY2 7BL - 01384 250333

THE WALK

Leaving the end of the canal at Stourbridge, walk to the main road and turn right. Shortly, the road bears left into St. Johns Road. Then the main road veers left: ignore this and walk straight on to the train and bus stations which are close together. Alight at Bishton Bridge on the A459 Dudley to Stourbridge road at the edge of Netherton. Cross the road and walk back to the bridge, turn left to gain the towpath, and left again, under the bridge.

Netherton to Park Head Junction - 2 miles

That most of the industry which made this canal such a busy route has now gone, replaced by smaller modern factories, is evidenced in the first few yards. Indeed, development proceeds apace, and walking the line every few months reveals more change.

This is a contour canal; patently obvious from the first few paces. With violent twists and turns, it contrives to stick to the level. Indeed, the skill of those early engineers can be appreciated when you realise that this Birmingham level, 453ft above sea level, is maintained through the tunnel, and back to Farmers Bridge Junction on the Birmingham Canal Navigations and then another 16 miles along the Worcester and Birmingham and Stratford canals to Lapworth. A total of 28 miles: quite a feat.

The towpath divides the canal from a large expanse of water at Lodge Farm reservoir which once fed the canal and where yachting and water skiing now provide entertainment for walkers. The ski jump is very close by. Beyond, the canal passes into a deep cutting. This was built as Brewins tunnel, named after one of the canal bosses, but was opened out in 1858. Housing now falls back from the water, and a degree of solitude can be experienced.

The first cast iron bridge appears around the corner, and it turns out to be just a narrow footbridge over a stump of old canal. This is Blackbrook Junction, where the 2 Lock Line, used to join the Number 1 Canal, cutting off the loop to Park Head Junction. Subsidence from the old colliery workings hereabouts saw the canal collapse at the end of the last century, and it was officially closed in 1909. Looking across the void to the other end of this branch a few hundred yards away and only 7ft lower brings the extent of the subsidence dramatically into focus.

The canal winds round

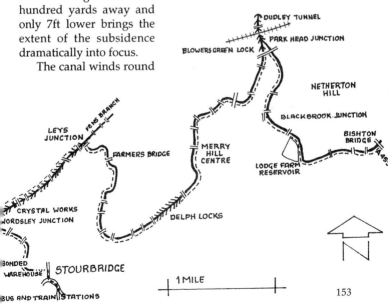

Netherton hill, with the church built right on the summit. A further $^{1}/_{2}$ mile along, Park Head Junction and the Dudley Number 1 Canal come into view. To the right are a couple of locks, and a short but very interesting section before the low forbidding entrance to Dudley tunnel. Crammed into these few yards you can see - if you stray that far - the remains of the Pensnett Canal (left) and the Grazebrook Arm (right).

Park Head Junction to Delph Bottom Lock - 2½ miles

The walk proper turns left, past the first lock, Blowers Green, which was rebuilt in 1893 replacing the bottom 2 of the Park Head flight. After almost a mile, Woodside Junction, the other end of the 2 Locks Line, is crossed by a bridge, and shortly after, the start of Round Oaks steelworks is approached.

The pitiful remains of this once great steelmaker are on the right, but amazing developments are around the corner: a mass of very attractive offices with construction and landscaping right to the edge of the towpath. Beyond Green Bridge on the left, the vast Merry Hill Centre is below the level of the canal. Known somewhat whimsically as Merry Hell to the locals, all the great High Street retailing names are there, with an overhead railway connecting. All very modern. A haulage yard on the right has its lorries arranged in serried ranks facing over the valley, whilst the box trailers, signwritten in huge letters, make an excellent advert.

Roughly halfway along the walk are the Delph Nine locks; but if you count carefully, there are only eight. There was a rebuilding programme here in 1858. The top and bottom were left untouched, but the middle seven were rebuilt as six to the west of the old ones. Once again, subsidence was the cause, but the need to completely resite was due in no small measure to the crucial role canals played in the industrial strategy of this area. To have rebuilt the originals would have meant closing the flight. An analogy of the chaos that would have caused would be closure of the M25 today for a couple of months or so.

This is now a Conservation Area, and traces of the old locks can still be seen. With the disappearance of one lock having taken place so recently(!) it's too much to expect the locals to start calling them the Delph Eight - yet.

Delph Bottom Lock to Leys Junction - 1½ miles

Beyond, the Dudley Number 1 Canal gives way to the Stourbridge
Canal. Here also the Portway Tackle Angling Club have the fishing
rights. They announce that this section is "PRIVATE, FOR MEBERS
[*sic*] ONLY".

Take care as you pass under Bretell Lane Bridge. It's very low,
and there is an obstruction on the towpath close to the water that is
difficult to see. In a house across the water here, the long garden is
given over to goats and vegetables.

As the canal takes a sharp left, there is an expanse of water to the
right. This was The Fens branch, a navigable feeder bringing water
to the canal from reservoirs on Pensnett Chase. Heading off to the
north-west a little further along was the Stourbridge Extension
Canal. This 2 mile canal was opened in 1840 to serve collieries and
ironworks in the area. It had two branches, and was progressively
closed up to 1960.

Leys Junction to Wordsley Junction - 1½ miles

The Stourbridge 16 locks follow. This area is being gradually tidied
and improved; a plaque on the wall surrounding the Sampson and
Lion pub indicates the inauguration of this project in 1990.

At Glasshouse bridge, a brief diversion can take you into the
Stuart Crystal glassworks. This beautiful cut glassware is typical of
the product that made this area famous. Refreshments and toilets
can also be found here.

The canal enters a particularly intimate length here with the
factory walls crowding in as lock follows lock in quick succession.
There is also a shop on the left selling the basics. A few yards beyond
the bottom lock, turn left into the Stourbridge Arm.

Wordsley Junction to Stourbridge - 1½ miles

Along here is a delightful brick built overflow. It's over 60ft wide,
but tapers rapidly to a 2ft channel crossed by the most intriguing
miniature canal bridge. Towards the end of the arm is a steel
founder who manufactures rainwater gullies and manhole covers;
they are stacked high behind a wire fence. Then, right at the end, is
the famous Bonded Warehouse. This was built in 1790 and enlarged
some 50 years later. The ground level was originally constructed in
an open fashion to allow bulk commodities to be unloaded from

boats into some sort of shelter. The building was restored, and is now used by the Stourbridge Navigation Trust, and the whole basin gives the impression of a canal community at peace in the midst of a very populated area.

WALK 30 - STOKE TO DROITWICH - WORCESTER AND BIRMINGHAM & DROITWICH CANALS

You are entering a particularly attractive corner of England now, with the opportunity to explore a length of derelict canal together with a stretch of highly popular cruising water.

There are actually three canals on this walk. The Worcester and Birmingham line opened throughout in 1815. It was a massive undertaking with 58 locks between the River Severn and Birmingham, all situated in the first $15^{1/2}$ miles: only six of them are included in this walk. The terrain also needed five tunnels. As the proprietors of the Birmingham Canal Navigations feared - see Walk 25 - the canal was very profitable, taking much trade from the Midlands to Worcester and reducing traffic on the rather more circuitous route to the Severn via the Staffordshire and Worcestershire Canal and Stourport.

In Worcester, warehouses at Diglis and Lowesmoor became important trans-shipment areas for many years. Trade took the inevitable nosedive with the advent of railways, and the company sold out in 1874 to the Sharpness New Docks Company. Several schemes were either considered or partially adopted to encourage trade, but it was all in vain. Cadbury's Chocolate were regular users of the line until the 1960s.

There were threats of closure made during the dark days of the 1950s, but they were stillborn, and the leisure revolution made the future of this attractive and challenging canal safe.

One effort made by the original owners to boost trade was to build the Droitwich Junction Canal. This ran from Hanbury and made an end-on junction with the Droitwich Barge Canal in the town. Opened in 1852, it was an attempt to tap into the lucrative salt trade, but never repaid the investment.

The Droitwich Barge Canal was a 7 mile canal from the town to the River Severn. Salt from the town was the primary cargo. There had been attempts to carry this trade by water for centuries. The River Salwarpe that runs through the town and into the Severn was the scene of attempted canalisation as far back as 1662; but with only limited success. A more effective water channel was needed, and the current canal was opened in 1771. It remained a busy line well into the last century. The Worcester and Birmingham Company bought the line and were then taken over by the Gloucester and Sharpness Company. Both lengths were abandoned in 1939.

In 1973 a Trust was established in the town to campaign for the reopening. Very little has been achieved yet on the Junction Canal, but the Barge Canal is navigable for some of its length. The locks at the lower end still need much work before the link to the Severn is remade. But, work continues and, funds allowing, success is eventually assured.

BEFORE YOU START

WALK DISTANCE:	5¹/₂ miles
MAP:	OS Landranger Series No 150
START:	Victoria Square, Droitwich
PUBLIC TRANSPORT:	Rail and coach services to the town
STARTING GRID REF:	SO 899635
CAR PARKING:	Several (pay) car parks around the town
TRANSPORT:	Midland Red West service 140 or 141 bus (not Sundays) to Stoke Works. Full details on 0345 212555
REFRESHMENT:	Everything in Droitwich, pubs at Stoke and Hanbury Wharf
NEAREST TIC:	St. Richards House, Victoria Square, Droitwich, Worcestershire WR9 8DS - 01905 774312

THE WALK

The bus leaves from Victoria Square. Alight at the Boat and Railway pub in Stoke. Walk a few yards north to the canal bridge on the right, cross and gain the towpath, heading back south.

Stoke Works to Hanbury Wharf - 3¹/₂ miles

A back view of the Boat and Railway is to be had. A pretty, but very narrow terrace with protection from the weather looks out over the canal. The houses on the far bank are old, but undergoing refurbishment. Wyche Cottages again indicate the presence of salt. The very name, Stoke Works, was applied to the huge brine pumping works established here in 1828. Much of the salt travelled by narrowboat in the days before railways took over.

Astwood comes and goes, although it is not easy to see where Stoke ends and Astwood starts. But beyond bridge 41 is the first of five Astwood locks. They are pleasantly remote from most things, except the Midlands to South-West railway, carrying high speed trains which rattle through at a frightful pace.

The old keeper's cottage is by lock 18, and one of the prettiest canalside gardens anywhere in the country is on the lockside. Systematically laid out with a vegetable patch which leads into flowers presenting a riot of colour, finished with a tiny lawn and exquisite rustic seat: spellbinding. Or at least it was in the height of summer. On a cold February day it could look a little different.

The large radio transmitter to the right may evoke some memories to older walkers. Who remembers the old Philco radios with a long wave dial for the BBC Light Programme marked "Droitwich" on the 1500 metre spot?

By the time the bottom lock is reached, the whole countryside has opened out into a series of gentle undulations; a charming scene of timeless quality. At bridge 35 leave

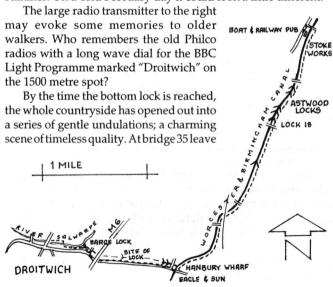

158

the towpath and turn right. The Eagle and Sun is a conveniently placed free house refreshment stop, selling Theakstons wonderful northern brews.

Hanbury Junction to Droitwich - 2 miles

A few yards down the road on the left is the Saraband Boat Centre, whilst on the right is access to the towpath of the Droitwich Junction Canal, and the top lock.

This length is weed free, well maintained and has a few boats moored. A coffer dam guards the approach to the first lock, which is gated, the only one on the flight. The chambers are very deep and in good condition. The reason this section survived when the ones lower down were lost is that the army used the area for many years as a testing ground for their equipment. Two more locks follow closely, and then: nothing. The way is barred, and the walk turns left to the main road, with the footpath becoming the "towpath" for the next mile. Turn right, but pause awhile to admire the view. Ahead in the valley is the delicate spire of the parish church pointing skywards whilst, beyond, the brooding hills at the far side of the Severn valley make a perfect backdrop.

The road, although undulating, is very straight. The reason for this is that it was once a Roman road called, appropriately, the Salt Way. After about 300 yards, search the hedgerow very carefully for a well concealed stone milepost with the legend B4090 Alcester 12 Droitwich 1. Behind that stone is a public footpath which gives access to one of the last narrow locks to be built in this country.

It's fairly decrepit, but worth the detour for historical reasons. But please take care. The path crosses a large garden belonging to the house close by. The lady there is a strong supporter of restoration: don't do anything to make her change her mind.

Continue towards the town, remembering that the canal was only a few yards away to the right. At the first set of traffic lights turn right, and just across the road is a large Landrover dealership. The canal starts again just to the right of this garage at Chapel Bridge. On gaining the towpath, turn right and walk for 100 yards to examine the remnants of Junction lock. Now well built over, this poses quite a problem for the restoration team. But, with increasing experience, solutions become ever easier: especially when the will and might of the local council are behind you.

Then resume the walk towards the centre of Droitwich. Ahead, taking the canal out of the River Salwarpe, is Barge lock. This unusual flood lock had gates that would swing both ways dependent on the state of the river. At the first swing bridge after the lock, about 50 yards away, cross to the far side to gain the towpath. This path skirts around the large basin area, at the far end of which is the rather grandiosely named Droitwich Marina: restaurant boat, one private boat, and one on the hard standing. Still, from little acorns...

Beyond is Netherwich Bridge. Pass under it, and leave the canal on the left, walking up to the road and the Railway Inn. Turn right and follow the road back to the town centre.